Read Write Inc.

Fresh Start

Handbook

Series developed by
Ruth Miskin

Revised edition

OXFORD
UNIVERSITY PRESS

OXFORD
UNIVERSITY PRESS

Great Clarendon Street, Oxford, OX2 6DP, United Kingdom

Oxford University Press is a department of the University of Oxford.
It furthers the University's objective of excellence in research, scholarship,
and education by publishing worldwide. Oxford is a registered trade mark of
Oxford University Press in the UK and in certain other countries.

© Oxford University Press 2022

The moral rights of the author have been asserted.

All rights reserved. No part of this publication may be reproduced,
stored in a retrieval system, or transmitted, in any form or by any
means, without the prior permission in writing of Oxford University
Press, or as expressly permitted by law, by licence or under terms
agreed with the appropriate reprographics rights organization.
Enquiries concerning reproduction outside the scope of the above
should be sent to the Rights Department, Oxford University Press,
at the address above.

You must not circulate this work in any other form and you must
impose this same condition on any acquirer

British Library Cataloguing in Publication Data

Data available

978-1-38-203522-4

3 5 7 9 10 8 6 4 2

Printed and bound in Great Britain by Ashford Colour Press

Acknowledgements

Illustrations: Tim Archbold

Photographs: by kind permission of Ruth Miskin Training.

Links to third party websites are provided by Oxford in good faith
and for information only. Oxford disclaims any responsibility for
the materials contained in any third party website referenced in
this work.

Oxford OWL

For school
Discover eBooks, inspirational
resources, advice and support

For home
Helping your child's learning
with free eBooks, essential
tips and fun activities

www.oxfordowl.co.uk

Contents

Getting started — 5
Introduction — 5
Fresh Start resources — 10
Route through *Fresh Start* — 11
Learn the sound system — 14
Manners matter — 16
Practice matters — 17

Assessment and progress — 18
Assessment Pupil Sheet — 20
Individual Record and Assessment Guidance — 25
Individual Progress Record — 28

Speed Sounds lesson plans — 29
Part 1: Set 1 Speed Sounds – single-letter sounds — 29
Part 2: Blending sounds into words — 34
Part 3: Word Time 1.1 to 1.5 — 35
Part 4: Set 1 Speed Sounds – Best Friends — 36
Part 5: Word Time 1.6 and 1.7 — 38
Part 6: Set 2 and Set 3 Speed Sounds — 39

Modules — 47

Introductory Module — 48
Timetable — 48
Activities for one-to-one tutoring — 48
Module-specific teaching notes — 52

Modules 1 to 33 — 55
Timetables — 55
Activities for one-to-one tutoring — 56
Homework — 61
Module-specific teaching notes — 62

Appendices — 128
Timetable and Module activities for a small group — 128
Glossary — 134
Simple Speed Sounds Chart — 136
Complex Speed Sounds Chart — 137
Red Words — 138
Summary of activity purposes — 139
Phonics practice activities for teachers — 140

Dear Reading Teachers,

Some students hate reading. They've left their book bags in the cloakroom all through primary school. They can't cut through the distractions around them and find it hard to pay attention. They skip over words they can't recognise, stumble through the words on the page – so many words to work out. Their anxiety about reading makes them freeze and so they stare at the pictures instead.

When a child first learns to read, they have to start from scratch, building new circuits in their brains. In the same way, learning to play the piano takes years of practice until your fingers work automatically and your mind is released to think about the music and make it come alive. Reading is no different. Students need a lot of carefully constructed practice every day. They need to put in the miles – the pages – to become readers. There are no short cuts, even if they are still learning to read at the top of primary or in secondary school.

So what are we waiting for? Given that students won't suddenly decide they're ready to read, we have to make them ready using *Read Write Inc. Fresh Start* – a carefully levelled phonics programme that is proven to get results.

It's human nature to love doing the things we are good at. *Read Write Inc. Fresh Start* will ensure your students are successful right from the start. And, the more *you* enjoy teaching reading, the more likely they are to enjoy learning to read. Students feel our passion for them – they know when we're on their side. They know when we will stick with them until they succeed.

Every school needs teachers who are passionate about getting students to read – teachers who will take up the challenge of getting every student to read. You!

Be prepared – the first year of teaching *Read Write Inc. Fresh Start* is the hardest while you learn the new systems. However, by the second year, you will have the confidence to teach any student to read and write.

I hope you will love teaching *Read Write Inc. Fresh Start* and share my passion for teaching students to read and write – particularly those who have been left behind to struggle for so long.

Best wishes,

Ruth

Introduction

Who is *Fresh Start* for?

Read Write Inc. Fresh Start is a fast-track catch-up programme for:

- Year 5 and 6 (P6 and P7) students who are reading below national expectations
- secondary school students who did not meet national expectations at the end of Key Stage 2 (P7) and older struggling students
- students with special educational needs and disabilities (SEND).

The lesson plans in this handbook and the training films on the Ruth Miskin Training School Portal (see www.ruthmiskin.com) show you how to implement the *Fresh Start* programme. They enable you to accelerate students' reading progress through the *Fresh Start* programme.

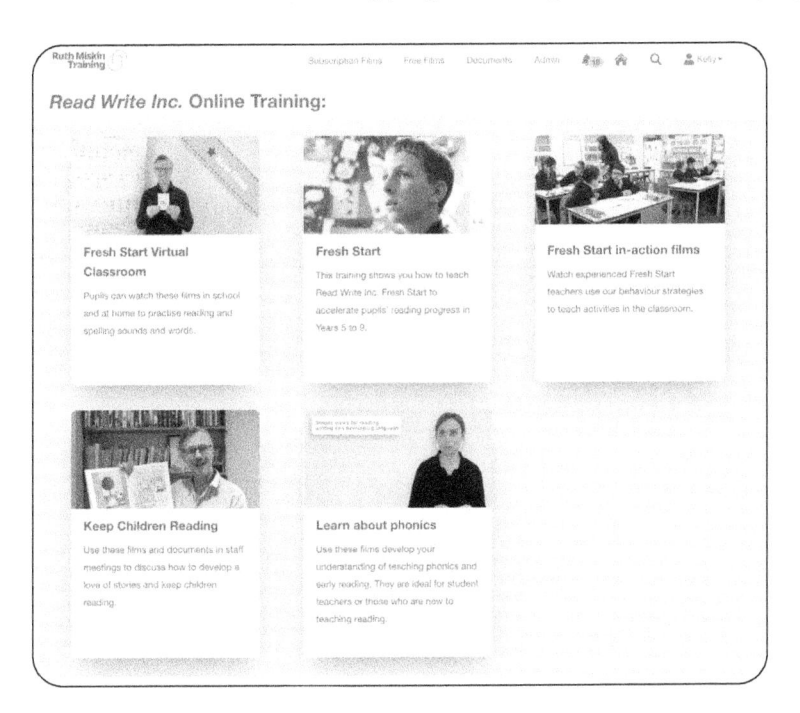

The role of the Reading Leader

Fresh Start is a simple, well-structured literacy programme. It is proven to raise standards in literacy rapidly when taught with fidelity and commitment. The programme should be run by a Reading Leader, who is vital in achieving this.

As Reading Leader, the key aspects of your role are to:

1. decide who will teach *Fresh Start*
2. organise training for these teachers/teaching assistants
3. support and practise with your team
4. assess reading every half term.

Getting started

What training is provided?

Online and face-to-face training is provided by Ruth Miskin Training (RMT).

Go to www.ruthmiskin.com to find out about training packages and costs.

The *Fresh Start* Online Subscription means that students can make faster progress. It keeps you up to date with the latest improvements because films are added throughout the year.

In this handbook, there are references to the training films (indicated by the film symbol ▶️) and these should be watched in conjunction with the teaching notes.

You can use the in-action films to watch experienced teachers teach every activity.

We suggest you watch the *Fresh Start* Getting started training films before you read pp.7–17.

What is the Virtual Classroom?

Teachers teach students directly in the Virtual Classroom films.

You can use these films in three ways:

- Use during lessons so you can assess students' progress and improve your teaching.
- Give students extra individual practice.
- Send home links to the lessons you have taught each week.

How can I build a team of excellent reading teachers?

Your aim as the Reading Leader is to develop a team who can work together, practise together, talk together and give feedback to each other. Plan a weekly/fortnightly 30-minute meeting so everyone can practise together. These meetings underpin the progress of all teachers and students.

Please give teachers/teaching assistants time to prepare for the lessons and to mark students' work. This should be at least 30 minutes a week, on top of the 30-minute weekly/fortnightly team meeting.

Getting started

How does *Fresh Start* work?

Fresh Start provides intensive, targeted support to address specific gaps in a student's reading.

Fresh Start teaches each student at their challenge point to accelerate progress. Students are taught to read sounds, words and the matched decodable Modules. The student learns to read the first set of sounds, and then how to blend the sounds together to read words. They then read simple texts containing the sounds they know, alongside learning more sounds, ready for the next set of Modules.

Throughout the programme, the student is taught the English alphabetic code – the 150+ graphemes that represent the 44 speech sounds. The most common 62 are taught in three sets of Speed Sounds (see pp.14–15). There are Speed Sounds Cards with simple mnemonics to help the student read and write the letter–sound correspondences quickly.

Stretch: mmmmountain
Handwrite: Maisie, mountain, mountain

The student practises reading these Speed Sounds every day until they can read them effortlessly. Then they can start blending the sounds together to read words. They begin by doing this orally, then they use the Speed Sounds Cards, and then progress to using the Green Word Cards.

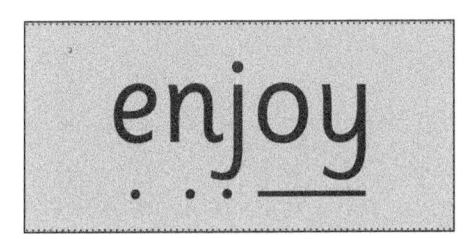

enjoy

When the student is reading the Green Word Cards, they are ready to begin reading the Modules. These contain decodable texts and activities for them to complete.

Read Write Inc. Fresh Start
Module 1
The Thing from the Black Planet

High frequency words that are not phonically regular are taught as 'tricky' words – we call these Red Words – and these are practised every day.

Getting started

How much time will I need?

20 to 25 minutes teaching time a day per student/small group. If a student is at the earliest stage of learning to read, they practise reading sounds and words for 20 minutes. This time is reduced to 10 minutes once they begin to read the Modules.

Sounds and words	Minutes	Modules	Minutes
Part 1: Learning Set 1 Speed Sounds – single-letter sounds	20		
Part 2: Blending sounds into words	20		
Part 3: Reading Phonics Green Word Cards: Word Time 1.1 to 1.5	20		
Part 4: Learning Set 1 Speed Sounds – Best Friends	20		
Part 5: Reading Phonics Green Word Cards: Word Time 1.6 and 1.7	10	Introductory Module	10
Part 6: Learning Set 2 Speed Sounds	10	Modules 1 to 3	15
Part 6: Learning Set 3 Speed Sounds	10	Modules 4 to 13	15
Knows Set 3 Speed Sounds	5	Modules 14 to 33	20

How long should students be taught for?

It depends on their starting place. Some students will only need a few weeks' tutoring. Others may need two/three terms.

Who can teach *Fresh Start*?

Students make rapid progress when they have individual support from an enthusiastic and well-trained tutor. This may be a teacher or teaching assistant.

Some schools choose one or two tutors who work with *all* students who need extra support. Others allocate students to one person who works in their class or year group.

Above all, tutors must be committed to teaching students to read – the student must know that the tutor is on their side and will stick with them until they succeed.

Tutors need to be available every day to ensure consistency and progress.

How many students can I tutor at a time?

For the initial Modules (until Module 13) we recommend that you teach on a one-to-one basis because students are at a very early stage of learning to read. Students who are tutored individually make speedier progress because you can target the tutoring specifically at their challenge point.

From Module 14 onwards, if you are unable to teach one-to-one, students can be taught in pairs or in a group of up to four, but only if they have been assessed at the same level. If a student makes faster progress, they must be allowed to progress in a group at the appropriate level.

How should I organise the teaching?

Organisation in primary schools

In Years 5 and 6 (P6 and P7), teach individuals or a group of up to four students for 20–25 minutes, either in the afternoon or in the morning instead of literacy.

Organisation in secondary schools

Either timetable one or two teachers or teaching assistants to teach *Fresh Start* students throughout the day. *Or* timetable teachers or teaching assistants to teach for the same half hour each day.

We recommend you avoid students consistently missing the same lessons.

How should I teach EAL students?

English as an Additional Language students who are new to English make speedy progress. Assess and teach according to their *phonic progress*. They must not be held back in the programme because they are new to English.

Students learning to speak English need plenty of practice in speaking and articulating their understanding. *Fresh Start* provides plenty of support to ensure EAL students comprehend the texts: a lively introduction to the story, explanation of new vocabulary on the back of the Module Green Word Cards, scaffolded questions to rehearse out loud before students write.

Getting started

Fresh Start resources

Core student resources	Additional student resources	Teacher resources
Introductory Module Workbook containing 17 short decodable stories/passages and activities.		***Fresh Start Handbook***: includes guidance for teaching the *Fresh Start* Modules, including the Speed Sounds lessons and Module lesson plans for each Module.
Modules 1–33 Workbooks containing longer texts, matched to students' phonic knowledge, and activities.	**Anthologies 1–7** For further phonic practice. (See pp.12–13 for more details.)	
Modules 1–5	Anthology 1	**Speed Sounds Cards, Set 1:** for teaching letter–sound correspondences, with simple mnemonics to help students remember the sounds.
Modules 6–10	Anthology 2	**Speed Sounds Cards, Sets 2 and 3:** for teaching letter–sound correspondences of the long vowel sounds and alternative spellings of long vowel sounds, with simple phrases to help students remember the sounds.
Modules 11–15	Anthology 3	**Speed Sounds posters:** for quick review of the letter–sound correspondences.
Modules 16–20	Anthology 4	**Phonics Green Word Cards:** for use in the Speed Sounds lessons, for students to practise word blending for reading.
Modules 21–25	Anthology 5	**Red Word Cards:** to help students read common words with uncommon spellings.
Modules 26–33	Anthology 6	**Module Green Word Cards:** to help students practise some of the decodable words they will come across in the Module texts and to provide definitions.
	Anthology 7	*Optional* **Picture Sound Cards:** with illustrated examples of words that start with the same first letter as the Speed Sounds, e.g. *m* for *moon*.

Route through *Fresh Start*

The chart below shows a summary of the progression of sound teaching in *Read Write Inc. Fresh Start*.

New Speed Sounds to learn	Speed Sounds to review	Progression of Modules	Anthologies for further practice
Set 1 Speed Sounds – single-letter sounds			
Blending sounds into words			
Phonics Green Word Cards: Word Time 1.1 to 1.5	Set 1		
Set 1 Speed Sounds – Best Friends	Set 1		
Phonics Green Word Cards: Word Time 1.6 and 1.7	Set 1	Introductory Module	
Learning Set 2 Speed Sounds	Set 1	Modules 1–3	Anthology 1 (texts 1–6)
Learning Set 3 Speed Sounds	Set 1 and 2	Modules 4–13	Anthology 1 (texts 7–10) Anthology 2 Anthology 3 (texts 1–6)
Knows Set 3 Speed Sounds	Set 1, 2 and 3	Modules 14–33	Anthology 3 (texts 7–10) Anthologies 4–7

For guidance on assessing and placing students precisely at the correct point in the programme, please see p.19.

The chart on the following pages details the progression of teaching in more detail.

Getting started

Overview of sound teaching sequence

This chart outlines the progression of sound teaching in *Read Write Inc. Fresh Start*. For example, once students have learnt all Set 1 Speed Sounds and can blend words made up of these sounds, they can start on the Introductory Module. When they move on to Modules 1–3, they are taught the Set 2 Speed Sounds and continue to review Set 1 Speed Sounds and blending.

Speed Sounds lessons	Modules	Focus sound(s) of the Module	Linked anthology texts from Anthologies 1–7
Set 1 Vowel sounds: a, e, i, o, u Consonant sounds: m, s, d, t, n, p, g, c, k, b, f, l, h, r, j, v, y, w, z, x, sh, th, ch, qu, ng, nk		*Additional sounds are circled on p.2 of the Modules. Sounds in brackets have already been taught.*	
	Introductory Module	**Speed Sounds Set 1:** a e i o u	
Students must be confident with all the Set 1 sounds before starting the Modules			
Revision of Set 1 sounds *plus* **Set 2** Vowel digraphs and trigraphs: ay, ee, igh, ow, oo, ar, or, air, ir, ou, oy	Module 1 The Thing from the Black Planet	**Speed Sounds Set 1:** a e i o u + CVC, CVCC and CCVCC words	1. Penpal from the Black Planet / Planets 'R' Us Travel
	Module 2 A wolf cub		1. Challenge Prof. the Boff! / Fang hunts with the pack
	Module 3 Big Malc		1. Hank Stock – strong man / Tests of strength
Students must be confident with all the Set 1 and 2 sounds before starting Module 4			
Revision of Set 1 and 2 sounds *plus* **Set 3** Alternative vowel sounds: ea, oi, a-e, i-e, o-e, u-e, aw, are, ur, er, ow, ai, oa, ew, ire, ear, ure, tion, tious/cious	Module 4 Hay into gold	**Speed Sounds Set 2:** ay	1. Six top tricks! / Inca bling!
	Module 5 Keeping a cat	ee	1. The day of the dog / Calling all dogs – the police need you!
	Module 6 Bill Bright's fishing trip	igh	2. High heels – or string vests? / Fish with Bill and Fred
	Module 7 The yellow light	ow	2. Know your fright limit! / Camping? Forget it!
	Module 8 Baboons on the loose	oo	2. Do you do zoos? / Top bananas
	Module 9 Bart the champ	ar	2. Fast track facts! / Speed, skids and mud!
	Module 10 Lorna	or oor ore	2. Stay cool in school! / Which school is for you?
	Module 11 A bad hair day	air	3. Lairy hair / Mrs Fairborn's baby
	Module 12 A good win for the red shirts	ir	3. What sort of football fan are you? / It's football – but not as we know it!
	Module 13 A player to be proud of	ou	3. Norman Knight, time-travelling superstar / Christmas 1914

Getting started

Speed Sounds lessons	Modules	Focus sound(s) of the Module	Linked anthology texts from Anthologies 1–7
Students must be confident with all the Set 1, 2 and 3 sounds learnt so far			
Revision and practice of Set 1, 2 and 3 sounds learnt so far		Speed Sounds Sets 2 and 3:	
	Module 14 Cook – and enjoy!	oy oi	3. Troy Tomato cooks up a storm / Unwrap – and enjoy!
	Module 15 Late	a-e (ay)	3. Room rage! / Get your skates on!
	Module 16 The weaving contest	ea (ee)	4. Peacocks or peanuts – Dr Dean looks at strange phobias / Monsters of land, air and sea
	Module 17 Amy Oliver's quick goldfish pie	i-e ie (igh)	4. Down the hatch! / Wild Mike's guide to staying alive!
	Module 18 Beep!	o-e (ow)	4. The phone zone / Home-grown sound effect zone!
	Module 19 Spellbound	u-e ue (oo)	4. Duke weds royal bride in wedding of the season! / Happy ever after?
	Module 20 The Outlaws	aw au (or)	4. Awesome! / The Fab Factor
	Module 21 Romeo and Juliet	are (air)	5. A fanfare for Monio and Oojilet / Once upon a love match
	Module 22 Sunburst Teen Magazine	ur er (ir)	5. Ask Shirley … / Many happy returns Sunburst!
	Module 23 How does it feel to be an astronaut?	ow (ou) e-e (ee)	5. A spell in space / They came from outer space!
	Module 24 Game raider	ai aigh eigh (ay)	5. Do it! / Shark for sale
	Module 25 Jason's quest	oa o (ow)	5. Left alone to die – The story of Alexander Selkirk / Extreme survival
	Module 26 New boy	ew (oo)	6. Keep fit for footy / New school blues
	Module 27 Kevin the killer hamster	er (ir) ire	6. The flight of Freddy Fish / The dog ate my homework!
	Module 28 Il Bello	_il _al _ve	6. Life on a cattle ranch / Watch that turtle hurtle!
	Module 29 A brilliant escape!	_ent _ence _ant _ance	6. Odd achievements / Emergency – the A and E department
	Module 30 Creature	ure _ture _ure _or _our	6. Creature features! / Monster
	Module 31 Macbeth	_ous _ious _eous _cious _tious	7. Superstitions – sense or nonsense? / A famous writer – Shakespeare
	Module 32 The invisible city	_able _ably _ible _ibly	7. A terrible day in Pompeii / Mission impossible!
	Module 33 Penalty for piracy: Execution	_tion _sion _ssion	7. Ballad of a pirate of distinction! / Pirate application pack
			7. *Extended reads*: Grand theft at Bagshot Manor / Survivors

Getting started

▶ Learn the sound system

Sounds

We use 44 speech sounds – 20 vowel sounds and 24 consonant sounds – to speak in English.

A 'speech sound' is a sound that changes the meaning of a word.

Take **man**: if you swap 'm' for 'p', you get **pan**. Take **fare**: if you swap 'are' for 'ire', you get **fire**. And in **shout**, if you swap 'ou' for 'or', you get **short**.

Different accents use different pronunciations of the vowels so it's best to stick with the student's accent, if you can, when pronouncing the sounds.

Letters

We only have 26 letters in the alphabet to write all the 44 speech sounds.

The sounds are sometimes written with one letter: 'c' in **cat**. Sometimes with two letters: 'ay' in **day**. Sometimes three: 'igh' in **night**. And even four: 'ough' in **thought**.

Some sounds are written in more than one way. For example:

- *ay*: day, apron, rain, they, make, eight, rein, straight, café
- *ee*: meet, seat, he, key, these, niece, funny, ceiling

To make it easier for students, we start by teaching just one way to read each sound. These are on the Simple Speed Sounds Chart on p.136. Once students can do this, they blend these sounds together to read simple words.

Then we teach students another way to read the sound, and then another until they can read the most common words in English. These alternative sounds are on the Complex Speed Sounds Chart on p.137.

We call words that contain common ways to read sounds: **Green Words**.

Some everyday words, however, contain an uncommon way to read one of the sounds. For example:

- **said**: 'ai' is very unusual – the sensible letter would be 'e'
- **the**: 'e' is very unusual – the sensible letter would be 'u'
- **your**: 'our' is very unusual – the sensible letters would be 'or'.

We call these **Red Words**. These are words that students often have to stop and think about, while they are first learning them.

There are a few Red Words that have an asterisk next to them. This indicates that the word is only 'Red for a while'. For example:

- **he** becomes a Green Word once students know that 'e' can represent the sound *ee*
- **go** becomes a Green Word once students know that 'o' can represent the sound *ow*.

Getting started

▶ Speed Sounds

We've organised the sounds into three sets:

- **Set 1**: consonant and vowel sounds represented by one letter:
  m, a, s, d, t, i, n, p, g, o, c, k, u, b, f, e, l, h, r, j, v, y, w, z, x
  and consonant sounds represented by two letters:
  sh, th, ch, qu, ng, nk

- **Set 2**: vowel sounds represented by two/three letters:
  ay, ee, igh, ow, oo, *oo*, ar, or, air, ir, ou, oy

- **Set 3**: alternative ways of spelling the Set 2 sounds:
  ea, oi, a-e, i-e, o-e, u-e, aw, are, ur, er, ow, ai, oa, ew
  and some new sounds and word endings:
  ire, ear, ure, tion, tious

We call them Speed Sounds because we need the students to read them speedily.

Pronounce the sounds clearly

When we teach sounds, we try to eliminate 'uh' at the end of the sound as this makes it easier to blend the sounds together to read the word. This is called the 'schwa' sound. We say '*c-a-t*' rather than '*cuh-a-tuh*'.

The top row of the Simple Speed Sounds Chart has the 'stretchy' consonant sounds. These are the sounds we stretch (just while students are learning them). It's easy to cut out the 'uh' in these sounds. For example: *mmmmmm, sssssss*.

Consonant sounds – stretchy

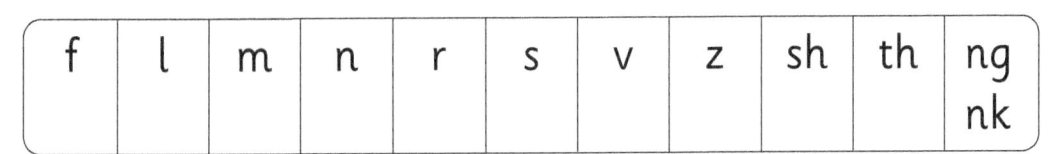

f	l	m	n	r	s	v	z	sh	th	ng nk

The second row of the Simple Speed Sounds Chart contains the 'bouncy' consonant sounds. You can't stretch these sounds, so we bounce them (just while students are learning them). For example: *p-p-p-p-p-p, d-d-d-d-d*. The schwa is easy to avoid on some bouncy sounds: *c/k, h, p, t, ch*. But harder with these: *b, d, g, j, w, y* (just take off as much 'uh' as you can).

Consonant sounds – bouncy

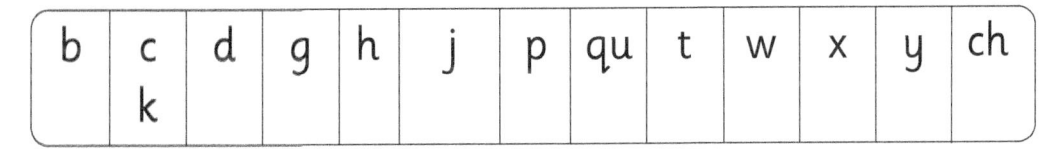

b	c k	d	g	h	j	p	qu	t	w	x	y	ch

The bouncy vowel sounds are *a, e, i, o, u*.

Make sure you can say the sounds clearly before you start teaching. The more clearly you say the sounds, the more quickly the student will learn them.

Sound Talk

Sound Talk is saying the individual sounds in the words. To help students read, the teacher says the sounds and then the student says the word.

For example: teacher says *c-a-t*, student says **cat**; teacher says *l-igh-t*, student says **light**.

See pp.140–144 for activities to help you practise phonics.

Getting started

🎬 Manners matter: mirror, model, mime

Students need to feel our commitment as tutors. Many have already failed. They need to know that we will stick with them until they can read.

Challenge point

We can only accelerate a student's reading progress when we find their challenge point each day – where the learning isn't too hard or too easy. After finding the right place to start, set *yourself* a challenge each day: What can I get the student to achieve in this session? Be ambitious – keep pushing on until the end of the session. If you go too far, take a step back so you can finish on a high note.

Mirror

- Some struggling readers are shy. For these students, we need to be patient, warm, gentle, calm, smiley – and importantly – quiet.
- Try not to be gushy or excitable. Avoid over-the-top praising, for example: Wow, Amazing!
- Some struggling readers look for ways to distract you, and themselves. For these students, we need to be all of the above, but also set strong boundaries.

Model

- We model exactly what we want the student to do before asking them to do it. Showing is much more powerful than telling.
- We gradually reduce the modelling until the student no longer needs any.
- If the first round of modelling isn't successful, we model again, and again. We do not resort to explaining.

Mime

- We avoid asking questions or narrating our modelling, such as, 'Would you like to…' and 'I'm now going to show you…'
- You will see how we model through mime, so instructions don't intrude on the modelling.
- We draw the student in with eyes and smiles.
- We mime how pleased we are when we succeed (in role of course) and when students succeed themselves, we use 'Thumbs up'.
- We will need to talk sometimes though, so don't feel you can't speak at all!

Where to sit

- Sit side-by-side on a straight table (not around a corner).
- Sit with your writing hand furthest away from the student.
- Try to be near in height (sit on a lower chair).
- Have your Speed Sound Cards and Green Word Cards ready to teach the Speed Sounds lessons.

Practice matters

Read Write Inc. Fresh Start has been crafted into specific steps and, like dance steps, they need to be practised before you tutor a student. If the steps aren't effortless, your effort will go into remembering them and not helping the student make progress. Students only make progress when you know the steps.

How to practise:

For each activity:

1. Read the steps
2. Watch the practice film
3. Walk through the steps
4. Practise in role – have an imaginary student next to you
5. Film yourself on a smartphone and check the steps are correct
6. Practise until effortless.

When effortless, watch the in-action film for the activity, to see how the teacher uses the steps to tutor the student.

Notice how the tutor:

1. Uses the steps fluidly, going back and forth when necessary
2. Mirrors the student
3. Models the steps
4. Mimes her praise
5. Challenges the student to achieve more and more.

Notice how the student:

1. Increases in confidence through the session
2. Makes significant progress in just one session.

Assessing students for *Fresh Start*

We can find a student's challenge point quickly using the *Fresh Start* assessment.

Please note: very important! We assess the entry point for a student by their word reading and fluency – not by their progress in comprehension or writing, or by their age. The reading activities ensure teachers support students' comprehension and students write at their own level.

Identify the right students for *Fresh Start*

In primary schools, assess all students in Years 5 and 6 (P6 and P7) who are reading below national expectations. In secondary schools, assess students who did not meet national expectations at the end of Key Stage 2 (P7) and older struggling readers.

Older struggling readers

If a student's reading is below what is expected for their age, it is important to determine whether they have difficulty with word reading (decoding), language comprehension or both of these, since different kinds of teaching are needed for each. The Simple View of Reading (below – Gough and Tunmer, 1986) can be useful when thinking about a student's reading difficulties and where they might lie in terms of three of the four quadrants.

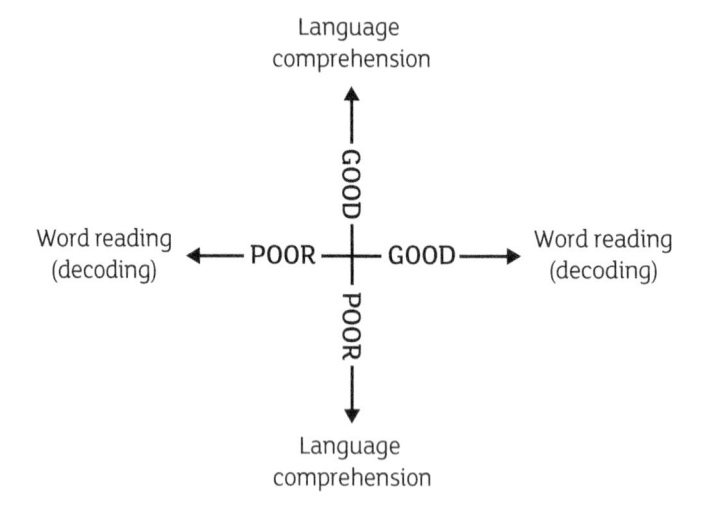

```
                    Language
                  comprehension
                        ↑
                        │
                       GOOD
                        │
  Word reading          │         Word reading
  (decoding) ←── POOR ──┼── GOOD ──→ (decoding)
                        │
                       POOR
                        │
                        ↓
                    Language
                  comprehension
```

Fresh Start accelerates reading progress for students who have good comprehension but poor word reading (the top left-hand quadrant), and those who have poor comprehension and poor word reading (the bottom left-hand quadrant).

Fresh Start is not for students who have difficulty understanding what they have decoded and good word reading skills (the bottom right-hand quadrant).

These students will benefit from teachers reading aloud to them every day to enhance their enjoyment of literature, increase their vocabulary and develop their language comprehension.

These students should read often, in English lessons and across the curriculum to:

- learn from their reading
- read for pleasure and for specific purposes
- become more fluent (with practice), since fluency is important for comprehension.

Ensure consistent assessments

Ensure the Reading Leader carries out all the assessments so they get to know the progress of all the students. It may, however, be necessary in a very large school to enlist the help of another teacher or teaching assistant. If so, agree how to annotate the assessments. Moderate your judgements by working together to assess a few students.

Assess the students

Download the following from the Ruth Miskin Training School Portal:

- Assessment Pupil Sheet – one copy of the assessment for each person carrying out the assessment (see pp.20–24 for Assessment 1)
- Individual Record and Assessment Guidance – one for each student (see pp.25–27)
- School Assessment Record (available online)
- Individual Progress Record (IPR) – one for each student (see p.28)
- Pupil Progress Tracker (available online)

Before you start, read the assessment instructions on the Individual Record and Assessment Guidance.

1. Ask the student to read the Assessment Pupil Sheet.
2. Use one Individual Record and Assessment Guidance sheet for each student. Mark off the sounds, words and passages they can read and then determine their starting point.
3. Count how many students are at the same challenge point and record on the School Assessment Record. Use this information to group up to four students together, if they have reached Module 14.
4. Transfer each student's starting point to the Individual Progress Record (IPR). Share with the tutor so they know what to teach. They will use the IPR to highlight the sounds, Word Time progress, Module and Red Words that the student has learnt to read each week.
5. Complete the Pupil Progress Tracker. Date the column corresponding to each student's assessment outcome to track individual progress.

Fresh Start Pupil Progress Tracker
Add each pupil's name to Column A. Date the column corresponding to each pupil's assessment outcome each half term.

Length of each lesson:									
Fresh Start lessons per week:									
Pupil's name	Set 1 Sounds – single letters	Blending	Word Time 1.1 to 1.5	Set 1 Sounds – digraphs	Word Time 1.6 and 1.7 (Intro Module)	Set 2 Sounds (Modules 1 to 3)	Set 3 Sounds (Modules 4 to 13)	Modules 11 to 15	Modules 16 to 25	Modules 26 to 33
Alison Pickford					07/09/2021			31/10/2021		
Pupil 2										
Pupil 3										
Pupil 4										
Pupil 5										

6. Repeat this process to assess and organise students for teaching every half-term.

Note that Assessments 1, 2 and 3 are interchangeable and it is important to rotate them. Assessment 1 is provided on pp.20–24. Assessments 2 and 3 can be downloaded from the *Fresh Start* pages of Oxford Owl (www.oxfordowl.co.uk/for-school/read-write-inc-fresh-start).

Assessment and progress

Fresh Start Assessment 1

Assessment Pupil Sheet

1. Set 1 single-letter sounds

m	a	s	d	t		
i	n	p	g	o		
c	k	u	b			
f	e	l	h			
r	j	v	y	w	z	x

2. Three-sound words

leg	cub
hat	sip

3. Phonics Green Word Cards (1.1–1.5)

lip	mud
sit	cup
pan	met

4. Set 1 Best Friends

sh   th   ch
qu   ng   nk

chunk   shin
sting   dish

5. Phonics Green Word Cards (1.6–1.7)

blob   spot
flop   trip
black   fluff

6. Set 2 Speed Sounds

ay   ee   igh   ow
oo   oo   ar   or
air ir   ou   oy

slay   steed
slight   flow
groove   hood
shard   thorn
flair   squirt
mouse   ploy

7. Set 3 Speed Sounds

ea oi a-e i-e o-e
u-e aw are ur er
ow ai oa ew ire
ear ure tion tious

plead   soil
glade   sprite
drone   crude
claw   snare
gurn   flutter
frown   claim
gloat   slew
retire   gear
fixture   prevention
ambitious

8. Passages

Passage 1 (Module 16)

Drink this …
Ha!
You are shrinking, shrinking …
You are as small as a pea.
Let me pick you up and put you on top of this beam.
Stop screaming. No one will come to help you.
Look – a skinny black leg!
Three – six – seven – and one more!
Start spinning, little one!
Spin, spin for the rest of your days!

Passage 2 (Module 26)

I'm in hospital. They're going to put a cast on my leg. They've said I can play football when my leg's healed. Some of the boys from school have been to visit me, which was really nice. They brought me some comics and loads of chocolates. It's funny – I'm missing being at school already. It is so boring lying here.

Passage 3 (Module 32)

We travelled towards open countryside outside the city. My cart was loaded with valuables, fruit and vegetables. I urged my donkey on. I knew he was capable of moving quickly over rough ground. But as we crossed the marketplace, where traders were packing up their stalls, the ground shifted beneath us.
I lost control of the cart and plunged forward.

Assessment and progress

Exit Passage (adapted from The Wind in the Willows *by Kenneth Grahame)*

They waited patiently for what seemed a very long time, stamping in the snow to keep their feet warm. At last they heard the sound of slow shuffling footsteps approaching the door …

There was the noise of a bolt shot back, and the door opened a few inches, enough to show a long snout and a pair of sleepy blinking eyes.

"Now, the very next time this happens," said a gruff and suspicious voice, "I shall be exceedingly angry. Who is it this time, disturbing people on such a night?"

"Oh, Badger," cried the Rat, "let us in, please …"

Fresh Start Assessment 1
Individual Record and Assessment Guidance

Student ....

Ask the student to read the sound, word or passage on the Assessment Pupil Sheet and mark them off here. Use the guidance in the assessment instructions column to determine the student's starting point.

Date	Assessment stage	Assessment instructions
	1. Can the student read Set 1 single-letter sounds? m a s d t i n p g o c k u b f e l h r j v y w z x	Ask the student to read the sounds. • If the student cannot read the first 16 sounds speedily, follow the steps in Speed Sounds: Part 1 (pp.29–33). • If the student can read the first 16 sounds, continue the assessment below.
	2. Can the student sound-blend three-sound words? leg cub hat sip	Show the student how you read the word **leg**. Ask the student to say the sounds and read the word. Ask the student to read the remaining words without your help. • If the student cannot read the words, follow the steps in Speed Sounds: Part 2 (p.34). • If the student can read the words, continue the assessment below.
	3. Can the student read Phonics Green Words Word Time 1.1–1.5? lip mud sit cup pan met	Show the student how you read the Phonics Green Word **lip**. Ask the student to say the sounds and read the word. Ask the student to read the remaining words without your help. • If the student cannot read the words, follow the steps in Speed Sounds: Part 3 (p.35). • If the student can read the words, continue the assessment below.
	4. Can the student read Set 1 Best Friends? sh th ch qu ng nk chunk shin sting dish	Ask the student to read the sounds and then the words. • If the student cannot read the sounds and words speedily, follow the steps in Speed Sounds: Part 4 (p.36). • If the student can read the sounds and words, continue the assessment below.

© Oxford University Press 2022. Copying permitted within purchasing school only.

Assessment and progress

Student ....

Date	Assessment stage	Assessment instructions
	5. Can the student read Phonics Green Words Word Time 1.6–1.7? blob spot flop trip black fluff	Show the student how you read the Phonics Green Word **blob**. Ask the student to say the sounds and read the word. Ask the student to read the remaining words without your help. • If the student cannot read the words, follow the steps in Speed Sounds: Part 5 (p.38) and teach the Introductory Module. • If the student can read the words, continue the assessment below.
	6. Can the student read Set 2 Speed Sounds? ay ee igh ow oo *oo* ar or air ir ou oy slay steed slight flow groove hood shard thorn flair squirt mouse ploy	Ask the student to read the sounds and then the words. • If the student cannot read the sounds and words, follow the steps in Speed Sounds: Part 6 (p.39) and teach Modules 1 to 3. • If the student can read the sounds and words, continue the assessment below.
	7. Can the student read Set 3 Speed Sounds? ea oi a-e i-e o-e u-e aw are ur er ow ai oa ew ire ear ure tion tious plead soil glade sprite drone crude claw snare gurn flutter frown claim gloat slew retire gear fixture prevention ambitious	Ask the student to read the sounds and then the words. • If the student cannot read the sounds and words, follow the steps in Speed Sounds: Part 6 (p.39) and teach Modules 4 to 13. • If the student can read the sounds and words, continue the assessment below.

Assessment and progress

Student ....

Date	Assessment stage	Assessment instructions
	8. Can the student read the passages?	Ask the student to read the first passage.
	Passage 1 (Module 16)	• If the student cannot read the passage in under 50 seconds, start by teaching Module 11.
	Drink this …	• If the student can read the passage in under 50 seconds, ask them to read the next passage.
	Ha!	
	You are shrinking, shrinking …	
	You are as small as a pea.	
	Let me pick you up and put you on top of this beam.	
	Stop screaming. No one will come to help you.	
	Look – a skinny black leg!	
	Three – six – seven – and one more!	
	Start spinning, little one!	
	Spin, spin for the rest of your days!	
	Passage 2 (Module 26)	• If the student cannot read the passage in under 40 seconds, start teaching Module 16.
	I'm in hospital. They're going to put a cast on my leg. They've said I can play football when my leg's healed. Some of the boys from school have been to visit me, which was really nice. They brought me some comics and loads of chocolates. It's funny – I'm missing being at school already. It is so boring lying here.	• If the student can read the passage in under 40 seconds, ask them to read the next passage.
	Passage 3 (Module 32)	• If the student cannot read the passage in under 40 seconds, start teaching Module 26.
	We travelled towards open countryside outside the city. My cart was loaded with valuables, fruit and vegetables. I urged my donkey on. I knew he was capable of moving quickly over rough ground. But as we crossed the marketplace, where traders were packing up their stalls, the ground shifted beneath us.	• If the student can read the passage in under 40 seconds, ask them to read the next passage.
	I lost control of the cart and plunged forward.	
	Exit Passage (adapted from The Wind in the Willows *by Kenneth Grahame)*	• If a student can read this passage in under 60 seconds, consider whether they would benefit more from taking part in full English lessons.
	They waited patiently for what seemed a very long time, stamping in the snow to keep their feet warm. At last they heard the sound of slow shuffling footsteps approaching the door …	
	There was the noise of a bolt shot back, and the door opened a few inches, enough to show a long snout and a pair of sleepy blinking eyes.	
	"Now, the very next time this happens," said a gruff and suspicious voice, "I shall be exceedingly angry. Who is it this time, disturbing people on such a night?"	
	"Oh, Badger," cried the Rat, "let us in, please …"	

© Oxford University Press 2022. Copying permitted within purchasing school only.

Assessment and progress

Individual Progress Record

Transfer each student's starting point to the Individual Progress Record (IPR). Ask tutors to highlight the sounds, Word Time progress, Module and Red Words that the student can read.

Student ....

Challenge point	Sounds and words	Modules
Learning Set 1 Speed Sounds – single-letter sounds	m a s d t i n p g o c k u b f e	
Blending sounds into words		
Reading Phonics Green Word Cards: Word Time 1.1 to 1.5	l h r j v y w z x Word Time 1.1, 1.2, 1.3 Word Time 1.4 Word Time 1.5	
Learning Set 1 Speed Sounds – Best Friends	sh th ch qu ng nk	
Reading Phonics Green Word Cards: Word Time 1.6 and 1.7	Word Time 1.6 Word Time 1.7	Introductory Module
Learning Set 2 Speed Sounds	ay ee igh ow oo *oo* ar or air ir ou oy	Modules 1, 2, 3
Learning Set 3 Speed Sounds	ea oi a-e i-e o-e u-e aw are ur er ow ai oa ew ire ear ure tion tious	Modules 4, 5, 6, 7, 8, 9, 10, 11, 12, 13
Knows Set 3 Speed Sounds		Modules 14, 15, 16, 17, 18, 19, 20, 21, 22, 23, 24, 25, 26, 27, 28, 29, 30, 31, 32, 33

Red Words

I my of the no to go all ball tall me said are was were you small want they call one what your do watch could their some there two does son love everyone water where would come here any caught should other who anyone people talk above through many brother thought bought whole walk father worse mother

Part 1: Learning Set 1 Speed Sounds – single-letter sounds

Start here if the student cannot read the first 16 Set 1 Speed Sounds.

Read the sound

Teach the single-letter Set 1 Speed Sounds in this order:
m, a, s, d, t, i, n, p, g, o, c, k, u, b, f, e, l, h, r, j, v, y, w, z, x.

Follow the steps below for the Set 1 single-letter Speed Sounds the student does not know. The tables on pp.30–33 give you a summary of these steps for each sound.

Review previously taught sounds and **teach two new sounds each day**.

1. Select a sound the student does not know (example: *a*).
2. Show the picture side of the card. Say 'Watch me copy our apple'. Draw a simple version of the picture on paper.
3. Trace your finger over the drawing (on the paper) as you bounce or stretch the sound (*a-a-a-a*) and say the picture name (apple) as you finish. Ask the student to copy.
4. Write the letter next to the picture on the paper.
5. Trace your finger over the letter (on the paper) as you bounce or stretch the sound (*a-a-a-a*) and say the sound (*a*) as you finish. Ask the student to copy.
6. Show that the picture side of the card matches your drawing, and the letter behind the picture matches your letter – 'same, same'.
7. Show the letter side of the card (*a*).
8. Flip the card from the picture side to the letter side as the student says the sound (*a*) when they see the letter and the picture name (apple) when they see the picture.
9. Mix the card with others the student knows and ask them to say the sounds speedily.

Next steps:

Review previously taught sounds and **teach two new sounds each day** until the student can read the first 16 Set 1 Speed Sounds speedily. Once the student can read the first 16 Set 1 Speed Sounds, follow the steps for Speed Sounds: Part 2 (see p.34).

Speed Sounds

Summary lesson plans for teaching Set 1 Speed Sounds – single-letter sounds

Sound	Read the sound
m (stretchy)	Draw Maisie and the mountains, then write m next to it.
a (bouncy)	Draw the apple, then write a next to it.
s (stretchy)	Draw the snake, then write s next to it.
d (bouncy)	Draw the dinosaur, then write d next to it.
t (bouncy)	Draw the tower, then write t next to it.
i (bouncy)	Draw the insect, then write i next to it.

Speed Sounds

Sound	Read the sound
n (stretchy)	Draw the net, then write n next to it.
p (bouncy)	Draw the pirate, then write p next to it.
g (bouncy)	Draw the girl, then write g next to it.
o (bouncy)	Draw the orange, then write o next to it.
c (bouncy)	Draw the caterpillar, then write c next to it.
k (bouncy)	Draw the kangaroo, then write k next to it.

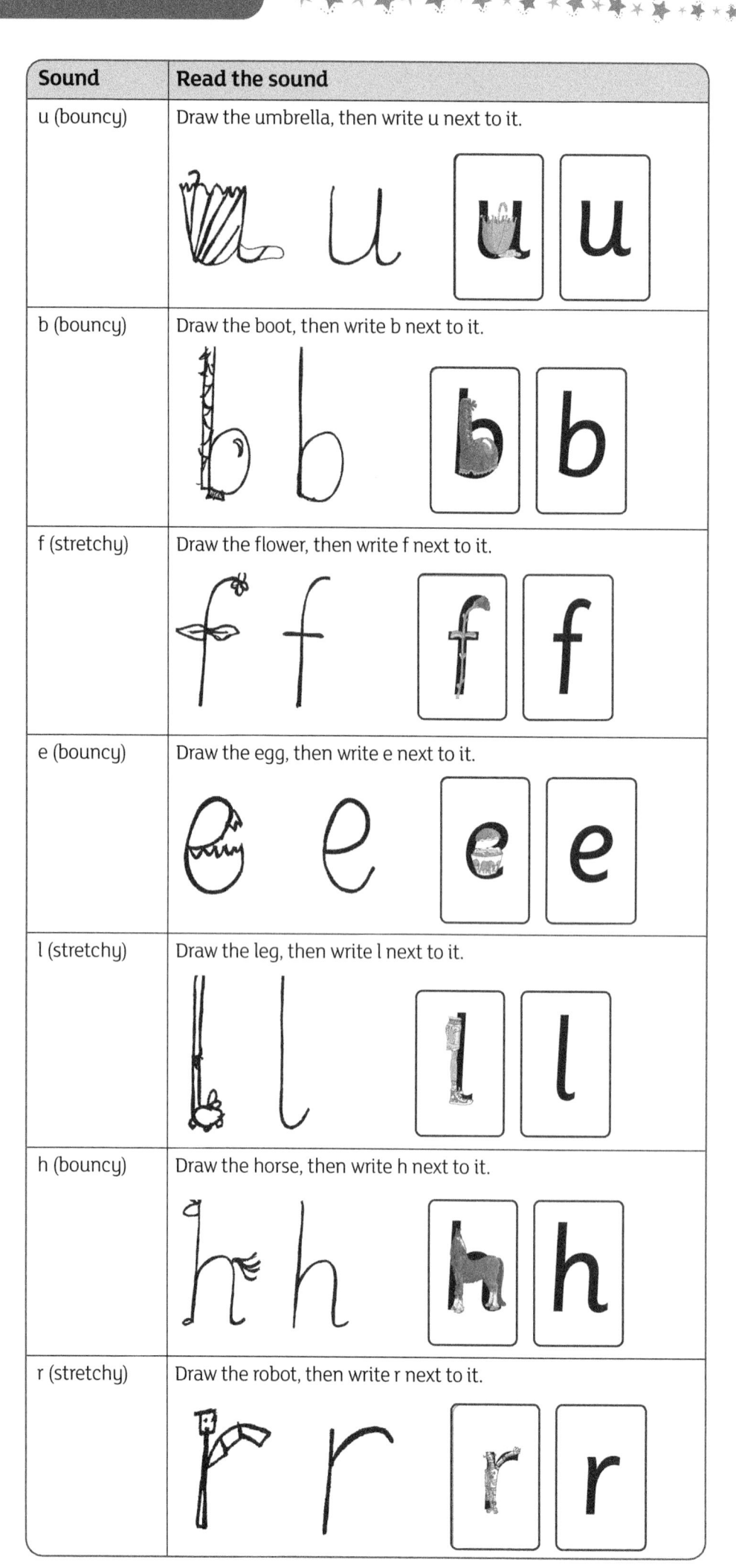

Speed Sounds

Sound	Read the sound
u (bouncy)	Draw the umbrella, then write u next to it.
b (bouncy)	Draw the boot, then write b next to it.
f (stretchy)	Draw the flower, then write f next to it.
e (bouncy)	Draw the egg, then write e next to it.
l (stretchy)	Draw the leg, then write l next to it.
h (bouncy)	Draw the horse, then write h next to it.
r (stretchy)	Draw the robot, then write r next to it.

Speed Sounds

Sound	Read the sound
j (bouncy)	Draw the Jack-in-a-box, then write j next to it.
v (stretchy)	Draw the vulture, then write v next to it.
y (bouncy)	Draw the yak, then write y next to it.
w (bouncy)	Draw the worm, then write w next to it.
z (stretchy)	Draw the zip, then write z next to it.
x (bouncy)	Draw the boy doing a star jump, then write x next to it.

Speed Sounds

▶ Part 2: Blending sounds into words

Start here if the student can read the first 16 Set 1 Speed Sounds speedily. All these steps are fluid – you may need to go back and forth between them until the student is confident.

🗣 Oral blending (no Speed Sound Cards)

Only use these steps if the student has significant difficulties blending with Speed Sound Cards.

Remember: only teach oral blending with sounds the student can read speedily.

Follow the steps below for the first 16 Set 1 Speed Sounds only. This activity is *without* cards.

Ask the student to look at you so that they can see your mouth as you Sound Talk (see p.15).

1. Select a consonant-vowel-consonant (CVC) word (example: pot).
2. Sound Talk the word in a slow, exaggerated manner (p--o--t). Show how you really 'think about' the sounds as you increase the pace of your Sound Talk and blend to say the whole word (p--o--t, p-o-t, pot).
3. Say the word in slow Sound Talk (p--o--t). Ask the student to copy.
4. Say the word in Sound Talk and the whole word (p-o-t, pot). Ask the student to copy.
5. Repeat the steps above for two more words.

[p][o][t] Blending with Speed Sound Cards

Remember: only teach blending with sounds the student can read speedily.

Follow the steps below for the first 16 Set 1 Speed Sounds only. This activity is *with* cards.

1. Select a CVC word (example: pot).
2. Say the word (pot). Say each sound as you make the word with the cards on the table between you and the student.
3. Point to and say the sounds (*p-o-t*), then sweep your finger under the word and say the word (pot). Slide the cards towards the student for them to copy.
4. Show the student how you play 'muddle, muddle': Place the cards in a different order in front of you. Say the word (pot). Drag the first card into place to make the word as you say the sound, and repeat for the next two sounds. Point to and say the sounds (*p-o-t*), then say the word (pot). Slide the cards towards the student for them to play 'muddle, muddle'.
5. Say the word (pot). Give the student the cards in their hands in a mixed order. Ask them to make and then read the word.
6. Repeat the steps above for four more words. Once you have taught a few words, aim to start at step 5 each time.
7. Make the word **met** silently with the cards – on the student's side of the table. Ask the student to say the sounds and read the word. Repeat with **dot**, **cub**, **pen**. If the student cannot read the words, repeat steps 1 to 6 until they can read the words without your help, starting at step 5 as soon as possible.

Next steps:

Once the student can sound blend, follow the steps for:

- Speed Sounds: Part 1: Learning Set 1 Speed Sounds – single-letter sounds (see pp.29–33)
- Speed Sounds: Part 3: Reading Phonics Green Word Cards: Word Time 1.1 to 1.5 (p.35)

Speed Sounds

Part 3: Reading Phonics Green Word Cards: Word Time 1.1 to 1.5

Start here if the student can read all the Set 1 Speed Sounds and can blend sounds into words using the single-letter Set 1 Speed Sounds.

Read Phonics Green Word Cards

mat

Remember: only read words with sounds the student can read speedily.

1. Show the student how to read two or three Phonics Green Word Cards using 'Sound Talk, read the word'. Use slow Sound Talk, and then speed up. Model until the student can jump in with you.
2. Give these cards and three others to the student. Ask them to read the words. If they need support, repeat step 1.
3. Muddle the cards and ask the student to re-read all the words.

Word Time	Sounds known	Words
1.1	m, a, s, d, t	mat, at, mad, sad, dad, sat
1.2	m, a, s, d, t, i, n, p, g, o	in, on, it, an, and, pin, pat, got, dog, sit, tip, pan, gap, dig, top
1.3	m, a, s, d, t, i, n, p, g, o, c, k, u, b	bin, cat, cot, can, kit, mud, up, cup, bad
1.4	m, a, s, d, t, i, n, p, g, o, c, k, u, b, f, e, l, h	bed, met, get, fan, fun, fat, lip, log, let, had, hit, hen
1.5	m, a, s, d, t, i, n, p, g, o, c, k, u, b, f, e, l, h, r, j, v, y, w	red, run, rat, jog, jet, jam, vet, van, yes, yet, yum, yap, win, web, wet

Next steps:

Once the student can read the 1.1 to 1.5 Phonics Green Word Cards, follow the steps for Speed Sounds: Part 4 (see p.36).

Speed Sounds

▶ Part 4: Learning Set 1 Speed Sounds – Best Friends

Start here if the student can read all the single-letter Set 1 Speed Sounds speedily and can sound blend.

Read the sound

Teach the Set 1 'Best Friends' Speed Sounds in this order: **sh**, **th**, **ch**, **qu**, **ng**, **nk**.

Follow the steps below for the Set 1 'Best Friends' Speed Sounds the student does not know. The table on p.37 gives you a summary of these steps for each sound.

Review previously taught sounds and **teach two new sounds each day**.

1. Select a sound the student does not know (example: *sh*).
2. Show the picture side of the card. Talk about the picture (the snake is making a nasty ssss noise and the horse tells the snake to shhhh), then say the sound and the picture phrase (*sh* – shhhh says the horse).
3. Ask the student to say the sound and the picture phrase (*sh* – shhhh says the horse).
4. Show the letter side of the card (sh).
5. Explain that the letters are Best Friends: two letters, one sound.
6. Flip the card from the picture side to the letter side as the student says the sound (*sh*) when they see the letters and the picture phrase (*sh* – shhhh says the horse) when they see the picture.
7. Mix the card with others the student knows and ask them to say the sounds speedily.

Next steps:

Review previously taught sounds and **teach two new sounds each day** until the student can read the Set 1 'Best Friends' Speed Sounds speedily. Once the student can read the Set 1 'Best Friends' Speed Sounds, follow the steps for Speed Sounds: Part 5 (see p.38) and start reading the Introductory Module (see pp.48–54).

Summary lesson plans for teaching Set 1 Speed Sounds – Best Friends

Sound	Read the sound
sh (stretchy)	Shhhh says the horse to the hissing snake
th (stretchy)	The person in the tower is rescued by the horse. They say: thhhhank you
ch (bouncy)	ch-ch-ch-choo! The horse sneezes when the caterpillar's hairs get up his nose
qu (bouncy)	qu-qu-qu-queen The queen takes her umbrella wherever she goes
ng (stretchy)	nnnng A thing on a string
nk (stretchy)	nnnnk I think I stink

Speed Sounds

▶ Part 5: Reading Phonics Green Word Cards: Word Time 1.6 and 1.7

Start here if the student can read all the Set 1 Speed Sounds and can read the Phonics Green Word Cards for Word Time 1.1 to 1.5.

Please note: While the student is learning to read the Phonics Green Word Cards, they can start reading the Introductory Module (see pp.48–54).

ship Read Phonics Green Word Cards

Remember: only read words with sounds the student can read speedily.

1. Show the student how to read two or three Phonics Green Word Cards using 'Best Friends, Sound Talk, read the word' (see p.134). Use slow Sound Talk, and then speed up. Model until the student can jump in with you.
2. Give these cards and three others to the student. Ask them to read the words. If they need support, repeat step 1.
3. Muddle the cards and ask the student to re-read all the words.

Word Time	Sounds known	Words
1.6	m, a, s, d, t, i, n, p, g, o, c, k, u, b, f, e, l, h, r, j, v, y, w, z, x, sh, th, ch, qu, ng, nk	ship, shop, fish, wish, thin, this, zag, zip, chin, chop, chat, quiz, quit, fox, box, fix, six, sing, bang, wing, wink
1.7	m, a, s, d, t, i, n, p, g, o, c, k, u, b, f, e, l, h, r, j, v, y, w, z, x, sh, th, ch, qu, ng, nk	3 sounds: bell, well, fell, huff, mess, sock, think, quick, thing 4 sounds: blob, blip, brat, drop, drip, clip, from, frog, flag, flop, grin, gran, pram, prop, slip, slid, skip, skin, spit, spot, stop, trap, trip, best, test, bend, jump, hand, send, dress, fluff, black, stink

Next steps:

Once the student can read the 1.6 and 1.7 Phonics Green Word Cards, follow the steps for Speed Sounds: Part 6 (see p.39) and start reading Modules 1 to 3 (see pp.55–67).

Part 6: Learning Set 2 and 3 Speed Sounds

Start here if the student can read all the Set 1 Speed Sounds and can read the Phonics Green Word Cards for Word Time 1.1 to 1.7.

Please note: While the student is learning to read the Set 2 Speed Sounds, they can start reading Modules 1 to 3 (see pp.55–67). While the student is learning to read the Set 3 Speed Sounds, they can start reading Modules 4 to 13 (see pp.55–61 and pp.68–87).

Read the sound

Teach the Set 2 Speed Sounds first in this order:
ay, **ee**, **igh**, **ow**, **oo**, *oo*, **ar**, **or**, **air**, **ir**, **ou**, **oy**.

Then teach the Set 3 Speed Sounds in this order:
ea, **oi**, **a-e**, **i-e**, **o-e**, **u-e**, **aw**, **are**, **ur**, **er**, **ow**, **ai**, **oa**, **ew**, **ire**, **ear**, **ure**, **tion**, **tious**.

Follow the steps below for the Set 2 and 3 Speed Sounds the student does not know. The tables on pp.40–46 give you a summary of these steps for each sound.

Review previously taught sounds and teach **one new sound each day**.

1. Select a sound the student does not know (example: *ay*).
2. Show the picture side of the card. Talk about the picture, then say the sound and the picture phrase (*ay* – may I play?).
3. Ask the student to say the sound and the picture phrase (*ay* – may I play?).
4. Show the letter side of the card (*ay*).
5. Explain that the letters are Best Friends: two/three letters, one sound. For *a-e*, *i-e*, *o-e* and *u-e*, explain that these letters are Best Friends, but they need to be split up because they are too chatty. They are two letters that make one sound, but they are not side-by-side.
6. Flip the card from the picture side to the letter side as the student says the sound (*ay*) when they see the letters and the picture phrase (*ay* – may I play?) when they see the picture.
7. Mix the card with others the student knows and ask them to say the sounds speedily.

Read Phonics Green Word Cards

Follow the steps below for each sound. The tables on pp.40–46 list the Phonics Green Word Cards for each sound.

1. Choose two Phonics Green Word Cards that include the focus sound (for example: play, way).
2. Show the student how to read the words (without dots and dashes) using 'Best Friends, Sound Talk, read the word'.
3. Give these cards and three others that also include the focus sound (for example: may, day, spray) to the student. Ask them to read the words. If they need support, repeat step 2.
4. Mix two of these cards with three other cards that include known sounds. Ask the student to read all the words.

Speed Sounds

Review the sounds

1. Mix the focus sound card with others the student knows and ask them to say the sounds speedily.
2. Keep a note of the sounds the student can't read and teach these the next day.

Next steps:

Review previously taught sounds and **teach one new sound each day** until the student can read the Set 2 and 3 Speed Sounds speedily. Once the student can read the Set 2 and 3 Speed Sounds, start reading Modules 14 to 33 (see pp.55–61 and pp.88–127).

Summary lesson plans for teaching Set 2 Speed Sounds

Sound	Read the sound	Read Phonics Green Word Cards		Review the sounds
ay	ay ay – may I play?	spray spray, play, day, way, may, say	Review words from Word Times 1.6 and 1.7.	ay
ee	ee ee – what can you see?	see see, three, been, green, seen, sleep	Review words from previous Set 2 lessons and Word Times 1.6 and 1.7.	ee
igh	igh igh – fly high	high high, night, light, fright, bright, might	Review words from previous Set 2 lessons and Word Times 1.6 and 1.7.	igh

Speed Sounds

Sound	Read the sound	Read Phonics Green Word Cards		Review the sounds
ow	ow – blow the snow	blow	blow, snow, low, show, know, slow	Review words from previous Set 2 lessons and Word Times 1.6 and 1.7.	ow
oo	oo – poo at the zoo	too	too, zoo, food, pool, moon, spoon	Review words from previous Set 2 lessons and Word Times 1.6 and 1.7.	oo
oo	oo – look at a book	took	took, look, book, shook, cook, foot	Review words from previous Set 2 lessons and Word Times 1.6 and 1.7.	oo
ar	ar – start the car	car	car, start, part, star, hard, sharp	Review words from previous Set 2 lessons and Word Times 1.6 and 1.7.	ar
or	or – shut the door	sort	sort, short, horse, sport, fork, snort	Review words from previous Set 2 lessons and Word Times 1.6 and 1.7.	or

Speed Sounds

Sound	Read the sound	Read Phonics Green Word Cards		Review the sounds
air	air – that's not fair	fair, stair, hair, air, chair, lair	Review words from previous Set 2 lessons and Word Times 1.6 and 1.7.	air
ir	ir – whirl and twirl	girl, bird, third, whirl, twirl, dirt	Review words from previous Set 2 lessons and Word Times 1.6 and 1.7.	ir
ou	ou – shout it out	out, shout, loud, mouth, round, found	Review words from previous Set 2 lessons and Word Times 1.6 and 1.7.	ou
oy	oy – a toy to enjoy	toy, boy, enjoy	Review words from previous Set 2 lessons and Word Times 1.6 and 1.7.	oy

Summary lesson plans for teaching Set 3 Speed Sounds

Sound	Read the sound	Read Phonics Green Word Cards	Review the sounds
ea	ea – cup of tea	clean, dream, seat, scream, real, please	Review words from previous Set 2 lessons.
oi	oi – spoil the boy	join, voice, coin	Review words from previous Set 2 and 3 lessons.
a-e	a-e – make a cake	make, cake, name, same, late, date	Review words from previous Set 2 and 3 lessons.
i-e	i-e – nice smile	smile, white, nice, like, time, hide	Review words from previous Set 2 and 3 lessons.

Speed Sounds

43

Speed Sounds

Sound	Read the sound	Read Phonics Green Word Cards	Review the sounds
o-e	o-e – phone home	home, hope, spoke, note, broke, phone	Review words from previous Set 2 and 3 lessons.
u-e	u-e – huge brute	tune, rude, huge, brute, use, June	Review words from previous Set 2 and 3 lessons.
aw	aw – yawn at dawn	saw, law, dawn, crawl, paw, yawn	Review words from previous Set 2 and 3 lessons.
are	are – care and share	share, dare, scare, square, bare, care	Review words from previous Set 2 and 3 lessons.
ur	ur – nurse with a purse	burn, turn, spurt, nurse, purse, hurt	Review words from previous Set 2 and 3 lessons.

Speed Sounds

Sound	Read the sound	Read Phonics Green Word Cards		Review the sounds
er	er – a better letter	never	never, better, weather, after, proper, corner	er
ow	ow – brown cow	how	how, down, brown, cow, town, now	ow
ai	ai – snail in the rain	snail	snail, paid, tail, train, paint, rain	ai
oa	oa – goat in a boat	goat	goat, boat, road, throat, toast, coat	oa
ew	ew – chew the stew	chew	chew, new, blew, flew, drew, grew	ew

Speed Sounds

Sound	Read the sound	Read Phonics Green Word Cards		Review the sounds
ire	ire – fire, fire!	fire, hire, wire, bon|fire, in|spire, con|spire	Review words from previous Set 2 and 3 lessons.	ire
ear	ear – hear with your ear	hear, dear, fear, near, year, ear	Review words from previous Set 2 and 3 lessons.	ear
ure	ure – sure it's pure	pic|ture, mix|ture, crea|ture, fu|ture, ad|ven|ture, tem|per|a|ture	Review words from previous Set 2 and 3 lessons.	ure
tion	tion – pay attention: it's a celebration	con|vers|a|tion, cel|e|bra|tion, ex|plor|a|tion, trad|i|tion, con|grat|u|la|tion, a|tten|tion	Review words from previous Set 2 and 3 lessons.	tion
tious/cious	tious – scrumptious; cious – delicious	de|li|cious, sus|pi|cious, vi|cious, pre|cious, fe|ro|cious, scrump|tious	Review words from previous Set 2 and 3 lessons.	tious cious

Introduction to reading the Modules

On the *Read Write Inc. Fresh Start* programme, students read stories and non-fiction texts that contain words made up of the sounds they can read. They know, that with only a little help, they will be able to read *every* word in *every* story you give them and, by the time they take it home, they will be able to read it confidently. They know that we will *never* ask them to guess a word, either from a picture or the context.

The early texts are *below* the student's comprehension level. (If you read the story to them, they would be able to understand it easily unless, of course, the student is new to English.) This is because they cannot yet read all the words they can speak.

Another point to remember is that most students cannot focus on the meaning of the story while they are working out the words. This is why we ensure students read the story twice: as their speed of reading increases, so does their ability to focus on what's going on in the story.

Before you start listening to the student read, it is really helpful if you practise reading the whole story aloud to yourself. This will help you introduce the story in an engaging manner and read it back to them in a storyteller's voice.

Always praise and encourage the student – they need to know that you care for them and that you will help them succeed. Frustration and irritation slows progress!

After the assessments, if you have to place a student on Module 13 or below, that student is at a very early stage of learning to read. Students at this stage will have very different gaps in their phonic knowledge and therefore teaching in groups is not recommended as you cannot teach at the student's challenge point.

For students on Module 13 or below, you should teach one-to-one wherever possible to ensure the fastest progress. The following notes are for one-to-one teaching. If you are unable to teach one-to-one, we recommend teaching students who have been assessed at the same level in a small group of up to four. See the notes in the Appendices (pp.128–133) for teaching in small groups.

Introductory Module timetable and activities

Introductory Module timetable

See timings on p.8.

Start reading the Introductory Module if the student can read all the Set 1 Speed Sounds, can read the Phonics Green Word Cards for Word Time 1.1 to 1.5, and is learning to read the Phonics Green Word Cards for Word Time 1.6 and 1.7.

The Introductory Module gives students practice in reading very short texts, to build confidence until they are ready to read the longer stories in Modules 1 to 33.

Follow the Speed Sounds lessons on pp.29–46. The Module activities for the Introductory Module are outlined in the blueprint teaching notes that follow. In addition to the blueprint teaching notes, some activities require Module-specific teaching notes, which are outlined on pp.52–54.

Complete one text over two days (there are 17 texts in the Introductory Module). However, if the student is making speedy progress, read one text a day. Each day's activities should be completed in 10 minutes (following 10 minutes of Speed Sounds tutoring).

This is a rolling timetable, so if you finish Day 2 on a Tuesday, start a new Day 1 on Wednesday.

Day 1	Day 2
Daily Speed Sounds lesson	Daily Speed Sounds lesson
Speed Sounds in Module	Green Words, Red Words and Challenge Words
Green Words and Challenge Words	Second Read
Red Word Cards	Questions to Talk About
Red Words	Hold a Sentence
First Read	

Introductory Module: activities for one-to-one tutoring

Speed Sounds in Module

Turn to the Speed Sounds page in the Module (p.2). Some sounds are circled on the chart. These are Best Friends that need extra practice.

1. Explain to the student that all the sounds in a box are the same.
2. Point to and ask the student to read each circled sound in and out of order.
3. Include other sounds the student needs to practise. Make it fun – get speedier as you point.

Introductory Module activities

▶ Green Words

Turn to the Green Words in the Module (on the same page as texts 1–11 and on the adjacent pages to texts 12–17). Note that the Green Words set in bold in the Module are the Module Green Words, which are available on cards.

Names and single-syllable words

For each word:

1. Ask the student to follow the routine: 'Best Friends, Sound Talk, read the word' (see p.134). Gradually, in later Modules, encourage them to read the word in their head.
2. Say the word again, using pronunciation that gives meaning if possible. Ask the student to repeat.
3. Explain its meaning in the context of the story if it is an unfamiliar word.
4. Ask the student to read the word again.

Multi-syllabic words

The longer Green Words are divided into chunks (syllables) by a grey line.

For each word:

1. Point to the first syllable on the page, covering the second/third syllable with a finger. Ask the student to read each part of the word. Only use the routine 'Best Friends, Sound Talk, read the word' if needed.
2. Say the whole word, tweaking the pronunciation if necessary, and using pronunciation that gives meaning, again where possible. Ask the student to repeat.
3. Explain the meaning in the context of the story if it is an unfamiliar word.
4. Ask the student to read the word again.

Root words and suffixes

For each word:

1. Point to the root part of the word on the page. Ask the student to read it in Sound Talk.
2. Ask the student to read the whole word with the suffix.
3. Say the word, tweaking the pronunciation if necessary, and using pronunciation that gives meaning, where possible. Ask the student to repeat.
4. Explain the meaning in the context of the story if it is an unfamiliar word.
5. Ask the student to read the word again.

▶ Challenge Words

Turn to the Challenge Words in the Module (on the same page as texts 1–11 and on the adjacent pages to texts 12–17).

For each word:

1. Explain to the student that the author needed to use a few extra words in the story with sounds that you have not taught them.
2. Ask them to see if there are any words they know.
3. Read each of the words to them and ask them to repeat.
4. If they forget them while they read the story, you will tell them the word.

Introductory Module activities

▶ Red Word Cards

Turn to the Red Words in the Module (on the same page as texts 1–11 and on the adjacent pages to texts 12–17). Collate the Red Word Cards listed and words from previous texts that the student needs to practise.

Give the cards to the student and ask them to read the words speedily. Put any they don't know to one side. For each word the student cannot read:

1. Hold up the card, for example: 'said'.
2. Say the word and ask the student to repeat it.
3. Point to the card and say the sounds you can hear, *s-e-d* and then say *said*. Ask the student to repeat.
4. Point out the circled tricky letters 'ai'.
5. Ask the student to read the word again.

▶ Red Words

Turn to the Red Words in the Module (on the same page as texts 1–11 and on the adjacent pages to texts 12–17).

1. Point to and ask the student to read the words. Encourage the student to read the words as quickly as they can. Repeat a couple of times.
2. Point to and ask the student to read the words out of order. Repeat until they can read all the Red Words at speed.

▶ First Read

1. Use the introduction in the Module-specific pages (pp.52–54) to introduce the text, without revealing the ending, to spark the student's interest.
2. Ask the student the introductory question on the Module-specific pages (see pp.52–54).
3. Ask the student to point to the words as they read. If the student gets stuck, prompt them to use Sound Talk to help them. (Do not ask the student to guess the words from the pictures.)
4. At the end of each numbered paragraph, read the paragraph back to them with appropriate intonation. (This helps them hang onto the storyline.)
5. Chat together about the characters and their actions.
6. When the student has finished, read the whole story to them, without asking for their help. Show your enjoyment.

▶ Second Read

1. Ask the student to read the story again, only using Sound Talk if necessary.
2. If the student still reads slowly, read the numbered paragraph back to them with appropriate intonation.
3. After reading each paragraph, chat about what's happening.

Introductory Module activities

▶ Questions to Talk About

Even though these are simple questions, below the student's comprehension level, they help the student notice what they've just read.

Turn to the Questions to Talk About page (on the same page as texts 1–11 and on the adjacent pages to texts 12–17). You will also find the questions on the Module-specific pages on pp.52–54.

1. Read out the questions. Do not ask the student to read the questions as many words are not decodable.
2. For each question, direct the student to the correct page to find the answer.
3. Some questions ask the student to respond using 'Fastest Finger', where they find the answer in the text and point to it. Others ask the student to 'Have a Think', where they have to justify their answer/opinion.

▶ Hold a Sentence

These sentences use words that the student has read. You will find the sentences in the Module-specific pages (pp.52–54).

1. Say the sentence and ask the student to repeat it until they can remember it.
2. Ask the student to write it in their Module on the same page as texts 1–11 and on the adjacent pages to texts 12–17.
3. Help the student to tick/correct each word and correct any punctuation.

Introductory Module

Follow the timetable on p.48. Use pp.29–46 to teach the Speed Sounds lessons. The Module activities for the Introductory Module are outlined in the blueprint teaching notes (see pp.48–51). In addition to the blueprint teaching notes, some activities require Module-specific teaching notes, which are outlined below.

First Read (texts 12–17 only)

Texts 12–17 can be introduced using the guidance below. (An introduction is not necessary for texts 1–11.)

12 Shopping list

1. Story introduction:

> Jan is at the shops. She's written a list of all the things she needs so she doesn't forget anything.

2. Introductory question: Which of your favourite foods would be on your shopping list?

3–6. Follow the remaining steps on p.50.

13 Help!

1. Story introduction:

> This text is a poem about a young boy. He's experiencing lots of strange sights, smells and sounds. But is he really in danger, or is his mind playing tricks on him?

2. Introductory question: What do you think it means if your 'mind plays tricks on you'?

3–6. Follow the remaining steps on p.50.

14 Fed up

1. Story introduction:

> Can you remember the last time you felt really fed up? This text is about a girl who's fed up with everything!

2. Introductory question: If your friend told you they were really fed up, what could you do to make them feel better?

3–6. Follow the remaining steps on p.50.

15 Packing

1. Story introduction:

> It's hard to remember everything you need to pack for a trip away. This text is a packing list of all the things Dan needs for his trip to Hill Crest Camp.

2. Introductory question: If you were going camping, what would you pack in your rucksack?

3–6. Follow the remaining steps on p.50.

Introductory Module

16 Simba

1. Story introduction:

> This text is about a lioness called Simba. She is hunting for food to give to her cub and she comes across a zebra.

2. Introductory question: Who do you think would win in a race, a lioness or a zebra? Why?

3–6. Follow the remaining steps on p.50.

17 Splash!

1. Story introduction:

> Do you like swimming? This text is a poem about a young boy who is swimming in the sea and imagines what he will see.

2. Introductory question: What do you think you would see if you swam in the sea?

3–6. Follow the remaining steps on p.50.

Questions to Talk About

1 Sick	How is the person feeling? What do you think is wrong with him?
2 Spin and slip	What do you think this person is doing?
3 Drink	What do you like to drink?
4 Get up	How is the person feeling? How do you know?
5 The shop	Where do you like to eat chips?
6 On a bench	Where is this girl sitting?
7 Puddle	How is the child in the puddle feeling? How do you know?
8 A black cab	What is the man wearing? What does the dog look like? What is the lad wearing?
9 In bed	Why is the boy in bed?
10 Red and pink fish	Describe all the different fish.
11 I am black	What is the animal? How do you know?
12 Shopping list	
Fastest Finger	Which items on the list could be eaten for: breakfast? lunch? tea?
Have a Think	Which are the unhealthy foods on the list? Which are the healthy items on the list?
13 Help!	
Fastest Finger	What can the narrator smell in his dream? What can he see? What does he touch?
Have a Think	Have you ever woken from a bad dream and not known where you are? What place could he be dreaming about?

Introductory Module

14 Fed up

Fastest Finger What is this girl fed up about?

Have a Think How fed up do you think she is?
Why do we not take her very seriously?
What sort of things put you into a sulk?

15 Packing

Fastest Finger Can you list all the things that Dan packs to eat?
Can you list all the things that Dan packs to wear?
What are the things that will keep Dan amused?

Have a Think Number the 5 most important things for the camp, in order of importance.

16 Simba

Fastest Finger What animal is Simba?
What is Simba tracking?

Have a Think Is it day or night?
How do we know the zebra is in danger?
Do you think Simba will catch it?

17 Splash!

Fastest Finger What can he taste?
What can he feel?
What is he imagining?

Have a Think Where is this person?
What sort of mood is he in?

Hold a Sentence

1. I am fed up and sick.	12a. Get me ten bags of crisps from the shop.
2. I can flip and flop.	12b. Pick up a big box of chocs as well.
3. Can I drink a cup of pop?	13a. Cobwebs brush my hand.
4. Run on the sand.	13b. I can smell damp, wet moss.
5. Can I get hot chips?	14a. I sit on my bed with the cat on my lap.
6. I sit on the hot bench.	14b. I will not help Dad with the dishes.
7. Run and jump in a puddle.	15a. Dan is off to camp with Ben and Sam.
8. I get in a black cab.	15b. Dan packs lots of socks and comics.
9. I am sick in bed.	16a. Simba trots in the hot sun.
10. A fish can swim.	16b. A twig snaps in the bushes.
11. I am big and I live in a shed.	17a. I think of a chest full of gold.
	17b. I sit on a flat rock with the sun on my back.

Modules 1 to 33 timetables

See timings on p.8.

Start reading Modules 1 to 3 if the student can read all the Set 1 Speed Sounds, can read the Phonics Green Word Cards for Word Time 1.6 and 1.7, and is learning to read the Set 2 Speed Sounds.

Start reading Modules 4 to 13 if the student can read all the Set 2 Speed Sounds and is learning to read the Set 3 Speed Sounds.

Start reading Modules 14 to 33 if the student can read all the Set 3 Speed Sounds.

Follow the Speed Sounds lessons on pp.29–46. The Module activities for Modules 1 to 33 are outlined in the blueprint teaching notes that follow. In addition to the blueprint teaching notes, some activities require Module-specific teaching notes, questions and answers, which are outlined on pp.62–127.

Day 1	Day 2	Day 3	Day 4
Daily Speed Sounds lesson	Daily Speed Sounds lesson	Daily Speed Sounds lesson	Daily Speed Sounds lesson
Speed Sounds in Module	Speed Words	Speed Words	Spelling – Green Words
Green Words	Red Word Cards	Second Read	Spelling – Red Rhythms
Red Word Cards	First Read	Questions to Read and Answer	Hold a Sentence
Red Words			Proofread
Challenge Words			
Speeding up word reading (this is an extra activity if the student's word reading needs an extra boost)			

As the student progresses, consider moving to a 3-day timetable (one Module over three days).

Day 1	Day 2	Day 3
Daily Speed Sounds lesson	Daily Speed Sounds lesson	Daily Speed Sounds lesson
Speed Sounds in Module	Speed Words	Speed Words
Green Words	Red Word Cards	Spelling – Green Words
Red Word Cards	Second Read	Spelling – Red Rhythms
Red Words	Questions to Read and Answer	Hold a Sentence
Challenge Words		Proofread
First Read		
Speeding up word reading (this is an extra activity if the student's word reading needs an extra boost)		

For homework activities and Anthologies, see p.61.

Modules 1 to 33: activities for one-to-one tutoring

Speed Sounds in Module

Turn to the Speed Sounds page in the Module (p.2). Some sounds are circled on the chart. These are Best Friends that need extra practice.

1. Explain to the student that all the sounds in a box are the same.
2. Point to and ask the student to read each circled sound in and out of order.
3. Include other sounds the student needs to practise. Make it fun – get speedier as you point.

Green Words

Turn to the Green Words in the Module (on p.3). Note that the Green Words set in bold in the Module are the Module Green Words, which are available on cards.

Names and single-syllable words

For each word:

1. Ask the student to follow the routine: 'Best Friends, Sound Talk, read the word' (see p.134). Gradually, in later Modules, encourage them to read the word in their head.
2. Say the word again, using pronunciation that gives meaning if possible. Ask the student to repeat.
3. Explain its meaning in the context of the story if it is an unfamiliar word.
4. Ask the student to read the word again.

Multi-syllabic words

The longer Green Words are divided into chunks (syllables) by a grey line.

For each word:

1. Point to the first syllable on the page, covering the second/third syllable with a finger. Ask the student to read each part of the word. Only use the routine 'Best Friends, Sound Talk, read the word' if needed.
2. Say the whole word, tweaking the pronunciation if necessary, and using pronunciation that gives meaning, again where possible. Ask the student to repeat.
3. Explain the meaning in the context of the story if it is an unfamiliar word.
4. Ask the student to read the word again.

Root words and suffixes

For each word:

1. Point to the root part of the word on the page. Ask the student to read it in Sound Talk.
2. Ask the student to read the whole word with the suffix.
3. Say the word, tweaking the pronunciation if necessary, and using pronunciation that gives meaning, where possible. Ask the student to repeat.
4. Explain the meaning in the context of the story if it is an unfamiliar word.
5. Ask the student to read the word again.

Red Word Cards

Turn to the Red Words in the Module (on p.3). Collate the Red Word Cards listed and words from previous Modules that the student needs to practise.

Give the cards to the student and ask them to read the words speedily. Put any they don't know to one side. For each word the student cannot read:

1. Hold up the card, for example: 'said'.
2. Say the word and ask the student to repeat it.
3. Point to the card and say the sounds you can hear, *s-e-d* and then say *said*. Ask the student to repeat.
4. Point out the circled tricky letters 'ai'.
5. Ask the student to read the word again.

Red Words

Turn to the Red Words in the Module (on p.3).

1. Point to and ask the student to read the words. Encourage the student to read the words as quickly as they can. Repeat a couple of times.
2. Point to and ask the student to read the words out of order. Repeat until they can read all the Red Words at speed.

Challenge Words

Turn to the Challenge Words in the Module (on p.3).

For each word:

1. Explain to the student that the author needed to use a few extra words in the story with sounds that you have not taught them.
2. Ask them to see if there are any words they know.
3. Read each of the words to them and ask them to repeat.
4. If they forget them while they read the story, you will tell them the word.

Speed Words

Turn to the Speed Words page in the Module (p.9 or p.10).

1. Point to and ask the student to read the words across the rows. Encourage them to read the word without Sound Talk if they can. Repeat a couple of times.
2. Point to and ask the student to read the words out of order. Encourage the student to read the words as quickly as they can.

Modules 1 to 33 activities

▶ First Read

1. Use the introduction in the Module-specific pages (pp.62–127) to introduce the text, without revealing the ending, to spark the student's interest.
2. Ask the student the introductory question on the Module-specific pages (see pp.62–127).
3. Ask the student to point to the words as they read. If the student gets stuck, prompt them to use Sound Talk to help them. (Do not ask the student to guess the words from the pictures.)
4. At the end of each numbered paragraph, read the paragraph back to them with appropriate intonation. (This helps them hang onto the storyline.)
5. Chat together about the characters and their actions.
6. When the student has finished, read the whole story to them, without asking for their help. Show your enjoyment.

▶ Second Read

1. Ask the student to read the story again, only using Sound Talk if necessary.
2. If the student still reads slowly, read the numbered paragraph back to them with appropriate intonation.
3. After reading each paragraph, chat about what's happening.

▶ Questions to Read and Answer

Turn to the Questions to Read and Answer page in the Module (p.8 or p.9).

1. Show the student how to complete the first question, and then ask them to complete the rest. Support if necessary.
2. The later Modules require a full response. Ask the student to read the questions and then, together, find and discuss the answers in the text. Choose one or two questions for the student to write full-sentence answers for.

▶ Spelling – Green Words

Turn to the Spelling page in the Module (p.7 or p.8).

1. Show how you complete a couple of words on the first grid and then ask the student to complete. Support only if needed.
   - Column 1: Dot the single letters and underline Best Friends
   - Column 2: Write the Best Friends – if there are any
   - Column 3: Write the number of sounds
2. Show how you complete the second grid. Explain how to split the word into the root and suffix.

The completed grids are provided in the Module-specific pages on pp.62–127.

Spelling – Red Rhythms

Turn to the Spelling page in the Module (p.7 or p.8).

1. Ask the student to read the first word, for example: said.
2. Read the word in sounds: *s-e-d*.
3. Remind the student which sound the circled letter/s represents: 'ai' represents the sound *e*.
4. Point to each sound as you say the letter name/s in a rhythm (exaggerating the tricky letters and then practise saying the rhythm together).
5. Close the Module and ask the student to write the first word.
6. Repeat with each Red Word.
7. Read all the Red Words in a rhythm again.
8. Close the Module and ask the student to write each word in their exercise book one-by-one.
9. Then ask them to tick/correct the spelling of each sound.

Hold a Sentence

These sentences use words that the student has read. You will find the sentences in the Module-specific pages (pp.62–127).

1. Say the sentence and ask the student to repeat it until they can remember it.
2. Ask the student to write it on p.7 or p.8 of their Module.
3. Help the student to tick/correct each word and correct any punctuation.

Proofread – spelling and punctuation

Turn to the Proofread – spelling and punctuation page in the Module (p.8).

1. Ask the student to follow as you read the sentences aloud.
2. Ask them to proofread and correct the sentences.
3. Ask the student to tell you the spelling errors. Ask them to tick/correct their work.
4. Re-read the sentences, exaggerating the sentence breaks and the effect of punctuation. Ask the student where they have placed the missing punctuation and to tick/correct their work.

Modules 1 to 33 activities

▶ Speeding up word reading

Once the student can read a word in Sound Talk, we then need to encourage them to read the word in their head. These steps help students who are reluctant to let go of vocal Sound Talk.

Read Speed Words

Write eight Speed Words from the Module onto cards.

1. Ask the student to read the words using 'Best Friends, Sound Talk, read the word'.
2. For longer multi-syllabic words, show how you work out the word by looking for Best Friends and identify familiar chunks, before you read the word.
3. Show the student how you read three words in your head, mouthing the sounds without speaking (maybe whispering to begin with).
4. Give the student all eight word cards to read (in mixed order). If they need more support, repeat step 2.
5. Muddle the cards and ask the student to re-read the words in their head, building speed each time.

Increase the speed

1. Show the student how to read three of the words speedily.
2. Give all eight word cards to the student to read. Repeat until speedy.

Challenge time

Only do this if the student has read the last set speedily.

Choose five new words from the Module.

1. Ask the student to read the words in their head.
2. Ask the student to read the five words speedily. Repeat.
3. Muddle the cards with the first eight word cards. Hold the cards and ask the student to read the words speedily.

Homework

Module activities

There are three types of Module activities that can be completed at home: writing tasks in all Modules, and – from Module 16 – vocabulary and grammar activities. These are available in the Modules, or if you'd prefer not to send the Modules home, you can download them as PDFs from the *Fresh Start* pages of Oxford Owl (www.oxfordowl.co.uk/for-school/read-write-inc-fresh-start). These activities are signposted in the Modules with the 'homework' icon, as shown below.

[H] Building vocabulary

1. Tell the student the focus word.
2. Read the sentence from the Module containing the focus word.
3. Use **TOL** (Think out loud) to build a sentence orally using the focus word.
4. Ask the student to use the focus word to build and write their own sentence at home. Remind them to use their phonic knowledge to help them spell words.

[H] Grammar practice

1. Read out the instructions in the Module for the Grammar practice activity.
2. Ask the student to complete the activity at home.
3. Mark the activity together the next day, correcting any misunderstandings.

[H] Writing task

1. Ask the student to turn to the writing task in their Module (p.10 or p.11).
2. For Modules 1 to 14: Point out the pictures showing the main events of the story. Explain that the student is going to use the pictures to retell the story at home. Point out that the first three pictures each have a sentence starter that the student can develop if they wish to. Alternatively, they can cross them out and use their own words.
3. For Modules 15 to 33: Explain the purpose of the writing task, for example to write a letter, a recipe or a report.
4. Draw the student's attention to the words in the Word bank, but also encourage the use of more adventurous vocabulary, even if they are unsure of the spelling. Tell the student to use their phonic knowledge when working out how to spell words. Accept phonically plausible spellings where alternative graphemes have not been taught yet. Note that if the student is likely to need more writing space, tell them to use the page in their Module to plan their response, and to write their full work in an exercise book.

Anthologies

The *Read Write Inc. Fresh Start* Anthologies contain a variety of non-fiction, poetry and fiction texts. They provide further practice of the graphemes students are learning and are intended to motivate them to read for pleasure outside of their *Fresh Start* lessons. See pp.12–13 for details of how the Anthologies should be used alongside the Modules.

Module 1

The Thing from the Black Planet

Follow the timetable on p.55. Use pp.29–46 to teach the Speed Sounds lessons. The Module activities follow the same steps for every Module. These steps are outlined in the blueprint teaching notes (see pp.56–61). In addition to the blueprint teaching notes, some activities require Module-specific teaching notes, which are outlined below. Answers to some activities are also provided.

First Read

1. Story introduction:

> Chip and Brad are two astronauts who are happily mending their rocket, the Sun Ship, when a hideous creature creeps up on them. Before they know it, the 'Thing' slings Chip across its back and runs off into the distance. Despite trying to catch them at Black Rock, Brad can do little to help his friend. When Brad sees the rocket lights flashing, he despairs. Will he get to the rocket in time before the Thing blasts off with Chip?

2. Introductory question: Have you ever tried to help a friend in trouble?

3–6. Follow the remaining steps on p.58.

? Questions to Talk About

Note: This activity is only for small-group teaching.

Fastest Finger	What does the Thing look like? (Section 1)
Read with Expression	How does Chip feel when the Thing grabs him? (*scared, worried*) Read his words aloud in Section 2, showing his feelings.
Have a Think	Why does Brad look grim? (Sections 2 and 3)
Fastest Finger	Where does Brad search? (Sections 6, 7 and 8)
Have a Think	Why did Chip rub his leg? (Sections 2 and 11)
Read with Expression	How does the Thing feel when it leaves the Sun Ship? (*embarrassed, annoyed*) Read what it did in Section 11, with feeling.

Spelling – Green Words

The completed grid should look like this:

	'best friends'	number of sounds		'best friends'	number of sounds
help	none	4	ship	sh	3
best	none	4	flash	sh	4
left	none	4	stomp	none	5
hand	none	4	crept	none	5
thing	th ng	3	much	ch	3
black	ck	4	rocket	ck	5
catch	tch	3	grip	none	4

Hold a Sentence

It was big and black with lots of lumps on its neck.

Proofread – spelling and punctuation

The correct text is: *"Hang on!" said Brad. "The rockets are flashing! The Sun Ship must be blasting off!"*

A | Anthology – further reading

This Module links to the following texts on pp.2–9 of Anthology 1.

Penpal from the Black Planet

1. Ask the student to turn to p.2 in their Anthology.
2. Introduce them to the text 'Penpal from the Black Planet'. Explain that this text is a series of messages between Rick and his penpal Zog, from the Black Planet.
3. Read the first page, drawing the student into the text so they will be keen to read the rest independently.

Planets 'R' Us Travel

1. Ask the student to turn to p.6 in their Anthology.
2. Introduce them to the text 'Planets 'R' Us Travel'. Explain that this text is a holiday brochure encouraging people to travel to the Black Planet.
3. Read the first page, drawing the student into the text so they will be keen to read the rest independently.

Module 2

A wolf cub

Follow the timetable on p.55. Use pp.29–46 to teach the Speed Sounds lessons. The Module activities follow the same steps for every Module. These steps are outlined in the blueprint teaching notes (see pp.56–61). In addition to the blueprint teaching notes, some activities require Module-specific teaching notes, which are outlined below. Answers to some activities are also provided.

First Read

1. Story introduction:

> Fang is a young wolf cub who is excited to be leaving his den for the first time. He journeys out on his own, experiencing different sights and smells as he trots around the rocky hills. It is only when Fang sees an unexpected visitor in the mountains that his adventure becomes a fight for survival.

2. Introductory question: Can you think of a time when you have been scared?

3–6. Follow the remaining steps on p.58.

Questions to Talk About

Note: This activity is only for small-group teaching.

Fastest Finger	Why do you think the wolf cubs can't go out hunting with their mother? (Section 1)
Have a Think	What do you think the cub feels as he stands outside the den? (Section 2)
Have a Think	Why do men want to kill wolves? (Section 5)
Read with Expression	How does the wolf cub feel as he hides from the man? (*terrified, anxious*) Read aloud Sections 6 and 7 with feeling.
Read with Expression	How does the wolf cub feel when he gets back to the den? (*relieved*) Read aloud Section 8 with feeling.

Spelling – Green Words

The completed grid should look like this:

	'best friends'	number of sounds		'best friends'	number of sounds
when	wh	3	lunch	ch	4
with	th	3	best	none	4
jump	none	4	trust	none	5
stand	none	5	quick	qu ck	3
next	none	4	strong	ng	5
think	th nk	3	smell	ll	4

Hold a Sentence

The man cannot get into this gap.

Proofread – spelling and punctuation

The correct text is: *The fluff on the back of my neck is standing on end. I wish I was back in the den with the rest of the cubs.*

> **A**
>
> ### Anthology – further reading
>
> This Module links to the following texts on pp.10–16 of Anthology 1.
>
> **Challenge Prof. the Boff!**
>
> 1. Ask the student to turn to p.10 in their Anthology.
> 2. Introduce them to the text 'Challenge Prof. the Boff!'. Ask them who they think 'Prof. the Boff' might be.
> 3. Read the first page, drawing the student into the text so they will be keen to read the rest independently.
>
> **Fang hunts with the pack**
>
> 1. Ask the student to turn to p.13 in their Anthology.
> 2. Introduce them to the text 'Fang hunts with the pack'. Ask them what sort of food they think the pack might hunt for.
> 3. Read the first page, drawing the student into the text so they will be keen to read the rest independently.

Module 3

Big Malc

Follow the timetable on p.55. Use pp.29–46 to teach the Speed Sounds lessons. The Module activities follow the same steps for every Module. These steps are outlined in the blueprint teaching notes (see pp.56–61). In addition to the blueprint teaching notes, some activities require Module-specific teaching notes, which are outlined below. Answers to some activities are also provided.

First Read

1. Story introduction:

> Big Malc is always trying to impress people, even if that means doing the wrong thing. In this story, Big Malc fools a shop assistant into thinking he wants an Elvis DVD for his mum. When the shop assistant's back is turned, Big Malc shoplifts what he really wants – a DVD of his favourite singer, Jon-Z. But when he brags about it to his best pal Snatch Smith, Big Malc realises that he is the one who's been fooled. What ridiculous plan will he think up next?

2. Introductory question: Have you ever tried to impress someone, even if it meant doing the wrong thing?

3–6. Follow the remaining steps on p.58.

? Questions to Talk About

Note: This activity is only for small-group teaching.

Have a Think	Why does Big Malc ask the man to get an Elvis DVD for his mum? (Section 2)
Fastest Finger	Why are the DVD boxes empty? (Section 4)
Fastest Finger	What went wrong with Big Malc's plans for the choccy eggs? (Section 5 and 6)
Read with Expression	What do you think Snatch feels about Big Malc? (*that he's not a very good crook*) Read aloud Section 6 with feeling.
Fastest Finger	What does Big Malc think about while he is in prison? (Section 7)
Read with Expression	What do you think Big Malc feels about himself? (*ashamed, embarrassed*) Read aloud the second paragraph in Section 7, 'He's planning ... Malc!'
Have a Think	Why does the story finish with 'I don't think so'?

Spelling – Green Words

The completed grids should look like this:

	'best friends'	number of sounds		'best friends'	number of sounds
spring	ng	5	stuff	ff	4
black	ck	4	melt	none	4
flash	sh	4	hundred	none	7
theft	th	4	quick	qu ck	3
think	th nk	3	rubbish	bb sh	5

root + ending	root	ending
boxes	box	es
nicked	nick	ed
planning	plan	ing

Hold a Sentence

Malc put eggs on a shelf but they melted.

Proofread – spelling and punctuation

The correct text is: *He's a big fan of Jon-Z. So off he trots to nick a Jon-Z DVD.*

A Anthology – further reading

This Module links to the following texts on pp.17–24 of Anthology 1.

Hank Stock – strong man

1. Ask the student to turn to p.17 in their Anthology.
2. Introduce them to the text 'Hank Stock – strong man'. Tell them that Hank Stock is also a shoplifter – but a different sort to Big Malc!
3. Read the first page, drawing the student into the text so they will be keen to read the rest independently.

Tests of strength

1. Ask the student to turn to p.21 in their Anthology.
2. Introduce them to the text 'Tests of strength'. Ask them to talk about any strong men or women they have seen perform on TV or in real life. (They don't have to be famous or a champion – they could be just someone they know.)
3. Read the first page, drawing the student into the text so they will be keen to read the rest independently.

Module 4

Hay into gold

Follow the timetable on p.55. Use pp.29–46 to teach the Speed Sounds lessons. The Module activities follow the same steps for every Module. These steps are outlined in the blueprint teaching notes (see pp.56–61). In addition to the blueprint teaching notes, some activities require Module-specific teaching notes, which are outlined below. Answers to some activities are also provided.

First Read

1. Story introduction:

> Kay's dad boasts to the king about his daughter's special skills. He tells the king that Kay can spin hay into gold, and the greedy king believes him. The king demands that Kay spins huge amounts of hay into gold before the sun sets, and threatens to kill her if she does not. An elf appears and promises to help Kay – but at what price?

2. Introductory question: Have you ever boasted about being able to do something?

3–6. Follow the remaining steps on p.58.

? Questions to Talk About

Note: This activity is only for small-group teaching.

Fastest Finger	Kay's father boasted to the king that his daughter had a special skill. What was it? (Section 1)
Read with Expression	How do you think Kay felt about her father's boast? (*angry, distraught, terrified*) Read Section 1 aloud, using an expressive voice for Kay to show her emotions.
Fastest Finger	What did the king threaten to do if Kay failed to spin the hay into gold? (Section 2)
Have a Think	Why do you think Kay agreed to pay him with a son, who had not even been born? (Section 3)
Have a Think	How did the king feel about having all that gold? (Section 4)
Have a Think	Do you think the elf was right to claim the child? (Section 5)
Fastest Finger	How does Kay trick the elf? (Section 7)
Read with Expression	How do you think Kay felt when she played a trick on the elf? (*pleased, happy*) Read aloud Section 8, using lots of expression to show Kay's feelings.

Module 4

Spelling – Green Words

The completed grids should look like this:

	'best friends'	number of sounds		'best friends'	number of sounds
sing	ng	3	grand	none	5
went	none	4	king	ng	3
hand	none	4	give	ve	3
trick	ck	4	neck	ck	3
fill	ll	3	stay	ay	3
way	ay	2	kitchen	tch	5

root + ending	root	ending
hopped	hop	ed
playing	play	ing

Hold a Sentence

Kay began to sob but then an elf hopped in.

Proofread – spelling and punctuation

The correct text is: *"Yes!" said the king when he saw it. He led Kay into a grand hall filled with hay. "When the sun sets, you must spin all this hay into gold," he said.*

Anthology – further reading

This Module links to the following texts on pp.25–34 of Anthology 1.

Six top tricks!

1. Ask the student to turn to p.25 in their Anthology.
2. Introduce them to the text 'Six top tricks!'. Ask them to talk about a trick that they have played on someone or have seen played on someone else.
3. Read the first page, drawing the student into the text so they will be keen to read the rest independently.

Inca bling!

1. Ask the student to turn to p.30 in their Anthology.
2. Introduce them to the text 'Inca bling!'. Ask them what they know, or can guess, about the gold in the Inca kingdom. (There were many gold mines/the empire was rich/ the gold was used for jewellery and statues/there was a temple made out of gold/the Spanish conquered the Incas because they wanted their gold.)
3. Read the first page, drawing the student into the text so they will be keen to read the rest independently.

Module 5

Keeping a cat

Follow the timetable on p.55. Use pp.29–46 to teach the Speed Sounds lessons. The Module activities follow the same steps for every Module. These steps are outlined in the blueprint teaching notes (see pp.56–61). In addition to the blueprint teaching notes, some activities require Module-specific teaching notes, which are outlined below. Answers to some activities are also provided.

First Read

1. Story introduction:

> Today, we're going to read a factual piece of writing about keeping a cat. Have you ever owned a pet? Do you have a pet now? Before you own a pet, you need to think hard about whether it is right for you and your family. You also need to know how to properly take care of it when it lives with you. This text gives information on how to look after a pet cat.

2. Introductory question: If you could have any pet, what would it be? Why?

3–6. Follow the remaining steps on p.58.

? Questions to Talk About

Note: This activity is only for small-group teaching.

Fastest Finger	What is the first thing you need to think about before buying a cat? (Section 1)
Fastest Finger	What is one of the advantages (good things) about getting a moggy or a stray cat? (Section 2)
Fastest Finger	Where will the kitten sleep? How will you look after its fur? How will it have fun? (Section 3)
Fastest Finger	How will you make sure the new kitten is happy? (Section 4)
Fastest Finger	Why is it important that you don't give the kitten titbits (extra bits of food for a treat)? (Section 5)
Fastest Finger	When should you take a kitten to the vet? (Section 6)
Fastest Finger	What should you do for your kitten if you go on holiday? (Section 6)

Spelling – Green Words

The completed grid should look like this:

	'best friends'	number of sounds		'best friends'	number of sounds
thing	th ng	3	greedy	ee	5
feel	ee	3	sleep	ee	4
keep	ee	3	holiday	ay	6
stray	ay	4	delay	ay	4
teeth	ee th	3	address	dd ss	5

Hold a Sentence

You will need a cat bed, feeding dishes, a tray and play things.

Proofread – spelling and punctuation

The correct text is: *A new kitten will sleep a lot. It may miss its mum. Tuck it into its bed. Pat it a lot. Do not let it get cold. Play with it when you can then it will feel happy.*

A | Anthology – further reading

This Module links to the following texts on pp.35–43 of Anthology 1.

The day of the dog

1. Ask the student to turn to p.35 in their Anthology.
2. Introduce them to the text 'The day of the dog'. Tell them that there is a well-known saying: 'every dog has its day'. Explain that it means that everyone is happy or successful at some time in their life. Ask the student to talk about what the text might be describing.
3. Read the first page, drawing the student into the text so they will be keen to read the rest independently.

Calling all dogs – the police need you!

1. Ask the student to turn to p.40 in their Anthology.
2. Introduce them to the text 'Calling all dogs – the police need you!'. Ask them to discuss how the police might use dogs to help them in their work.
3. Read the first page, drawing the student into the text so they will be keen to read the rest independently.

Module 6

Bill Bright's fishing trip

Follow the timetable on p.55. Use pp.29–46 to teach the Speed Sounds lessons. The Module activities follow the same steps for every Module. These steps are outlined in the blueprint teaching notes (see pp.56–61). In addition to the blueprint teaching notes, some activities require Module-specific teaching notes, which are outlined below. Answers to some activities are also provided.

First Read

1. Story introduction:

> Bill Bright lives on his own in a small flat on the Isle of Wight. He decides to take a trip to High Springs in Florida, USA, to spend a holiday doing what he loves – fishing! Bill is happy and excited. It is the first time he has ever been on an aeroplane. Bill enjoys the flight and can't wait to go fishing, but he has a big shock when he gets to his hotel.

2. Introductory question: Have you ever been really excited about going somewhere? Where did you go?

3–6. Follow the remaining steps on p.58.

Questions to Talk About

Note: This activity is only for small-group teaching.

Have a Think	Why do you think Bill needs a new bag? (Section 1)
Read with Expression	How does he feel when he sees his bag going past on a truck? (*proud, excited*) Read aloud Section 2, speaking as Bill with feeling and expression.
Have a Think	Why did the men on the runway seem small? (Section 3)
Fastest Finger	What did Bill see out of the window during the night? (Section 4)
Have a Think	Why didn't Bill check the address on his bag? (Section 5)
Read with Expression	What do you think Bill feels when he opens the case in the hotel? (*surprised, shocked, embarrassed, foolish*) Read aloud Section 6, with feeling and expression to echo Bill's feelings.

Spelling – Green Words

The completed grids should look like this:

	'best friends'	number of sounds		'best friends'	number of sounds
slight	igh	4	fantastic	none	9
green	ee	4	holiday	ay	6
flight	igh	4	fright	igh	4
lightning	igh ng	6	address	dd ss	5

root + ending	root	ending
gasping	gasp	ing
gasped	gasp	ed
slammed	slam	ed

Hold a Sentence

He went to the shops and got a bright green bag.

Proofread – spelling and punctuation

The correct text is: Bill got to the jet on a bus. He watched all the bags going past on a truck. "I can see my bright green bag!" he said to himself with a grin.

> ### Anthology – further reading
>
> This Module links to the following texts on pp.2–10 of Anthology 2.
>
> **High heels – or string vests?**
>
> 1. Ask the student to turn to p.2 in their Anthology.
> 2. Introduce them to the text 'High heels – or string vests?'. Explain that, in this text, several passengers have had their bags mixed up and they will need to work out which bag belongs to which passenger.
> 3. Read the first page, drawing the student into the text so they will be keen to read the rest independently.
>
> **Fish with Bill and Fred**
>
> 1. Ask the student to turn to p.7 in their Anthology.
> 2. Introduce them to the text 'Fish with Bill and Fred'. Explain that this advice text is written by two fishermen: Bill, who is an expert, and Fred, who is not!
> 3. Read the first page, drawing the student into the text so they will be keen to read the rest independently.

Module 7

The yellow light

Follow the timetable on p.55. Use pp.29–46 to teach the Speed Sounds lessons. The Module activities follow the same steps for every Module. These steps are outlined in the blueprint teaching notes (see pp.56–61). In addition to the blueprint teaching notes, some activities require Module-specific teaching notes, which are outlined below. Answers to some activities are also provided.

First Read

1. Story introduction:

> The children in this story are on a school camping trip. Ella is ready to go home. Although she's sharing a tent with her best friend, Willow, she is not happy. She is sick of the trees, sick of washing up, and especially sick of Jack Haddow being childish all the time. Most of all, however, she is scared of sleeping in the tent. One night, she hears strange noises and sees a yellow light glowing on the canvas of the tent. She hopes it is just Miss Owen checking on them and decides to take a closer look.

2. Introductory question: Have you been away with your school? Were you homesick?

3–6. Follow the remaining steps on p.58.

Questions to Talk About

Note: This activity is only for small-group teaching.

Fastest Finger	Who was Ella sharing a tent with? (Section 1)
Have a Think	Why was Ella tired of camping? (Section 2)
Read with Expression	How do you think Ella felt when she thought she heard a ghost? (*scared, nervous, terrified*) Read Section 3 aloud, showing her feelings.
Read with Expression	What did Ella see among the trees? Read the description in Section 4 aloud, in a spooky voice.
Fastest Finger	What did Ella see that makes her realise there wasn't really a ghost? (Section 5)
Read with Expression	How did Ella feel when she knew who the ghost was? (*relieved, cross, amused, clever*) Read aloud what she said to the ghost in Section 5, showing her feelings.
Have a Think	What do you think Ella really feels about Jack Haddow? (Section 6)

Spelling – Green Words

The completed grids should look like this:

	'best friends'	number of sounds		'best friends'	number of sounds
kn ow	kn ow	2	fl ow	ow	3
sh ow	sh ow	2	bell ow	ll ow	4
narr ow	rr ow	4	yell ow	ll ow	4
shadow	sh ow	4	foll ow	ll ow	4

root + ending	root	ending
gripped	grip	ed
screeched	screech	ed
bellowed	bellow	ed
borrowed	borrow	ed

Hold a Sentence

Ella was sick of Jack Haddow. He was a show off.

Proofread – spelling and punctuation

The correct text is: *A shadow danced in the trees. Its long, flowing dress seemed to shed ghostly rays and its elbows flapped in and out. The yellow light danced as well and seemed to grow brighter.*

A | Anthology – further reading

This Module links to the following texts on pp.11–17 of Anthology 2.

Know your fright limit!
1. Ask the student to turn to p.11 in their Anthology.
2. Introduce them to the text 'Know your fright limit!'. Explain that the text is a quiz that they can use to find out what their 'fright limit' is.
3. Read the introduction and explain how the 'fright limit' is rated by the ghost symbols. Ask the student to do the quiz in their own time.

Camping? Forget it!
1. Ask the student to turn to p.14 in their Anthology.
2. Introduce them to the text 'Camping? Forget it!'. Explain that you have had mixed experiences when camping – some good, some bad, providing an example of each. Ask them to discuss what they think (or know) they would enjoy about camping and what they might hate.
3. Read the first page, drawing the student into the text so they will be keen to read the rest independently.

Module 8

Baboons on the loose

Follow the timetable on p.55. Use pp.29–46 to teach the Speed Sounds lessons. The Module activities follow the same steps for every Module. These steps are outlined in the blueprint teaching notes (see pp.56–61). In addition to the blueprint teaching notes, some activities require Module-specific teaching notes, which are outlined below. Answers to some activities are also provided.

First Read

1. Story introduction:

> The children in this story are on a school trip at the zoo. Mr Moon has set them the task of choosing an animal to write about. Ella and Willow quickly get bored, but their classmate Jay Rooney is working so hard he needs extra paper! Needless to say, Jack Haddow does not do as he is told, and in the end, gets the whole class sent home early. But what exactly did he do?

2. Introductory question: Have you ever been to the zoo? Which animals did you think were the most amusing?

3–6. Follow the remaining steps on p.58.

⟨?⟩ Questions to Talk About

Note: This activity is only for small-group teaching.

Have a Think	What was Mr Moon's joke about 'living things'? (Section 1)
Fastest Finger	What question did Mr Moon ask Ella? (Section 2)
Have a Think	Why did Mr Moon say 'Um ... yes' even when Jack gives a correct answer? (Section 4)
Read with Expression	How did Willow feel about the task Mr Moon gives them? (*boring, dull, difficult*) Read aloud Section 7, speaking Willow's words with feeling.
Have a Think	What was Jack curious about? (Section 9)
Read with Expression	What does Mr Moon feel about Jack? (*exasperated, disappointed, frustrated*) Read Section 11 aloud, speaking Mr Moon's words with feeling.

Spelling – Green Words

The completed grids should look like this:

	'best friends'	number of sounds		'best friends'	number of sounds
ch oo se	ch oo se	3	classroom	ss oo	7
loo se	oo se	3	kangaroo	ng oo	6
sch ool	ch oo	4	window	ow	5
fool	oo	3	animal	none	6

root + ending	root	ending
boomed	boom	ed
living	live	ing
sighed	sigh	ed
sitting	sit	ing

Hold a Sentence

Willow put down one fact about the food.

Proofread – spelling and punctuation

The correct text is: *Jack Haddow went to look at the baboons. One was grooming a baby, and one was scooping up handfuls of food from a tub. "What is that?" said Jack.*

A | Anthology – further reading

This Module links to the following texts on pp.18–26 of Anthology 2.

Do you do zoos?

1. Ask the student to turn to p.18 in their Anthology.
2. Introduce them to the text 'Do you do zoos?'. Ensure they understand this is about two people (Jay and Jools) putting forward different views about zoos. Point out that there are also two poems written from the viewpoint of two orang-utans, one living in a zoo, the other in a tropical rainforest. Write the word 'Orang-utan'. Ask the student to say the sounds, then say the whole word. Use My turn Your turn (see p.134) to repeat the word.
3. Read the introduction, drawing the student into the text so they will be keen to read the rest independently.

Top bananas

1. Ask the student to turn to p.22 in their Anthology.
2. Introduce them to the text 'Top bananas'. Ask them what they know about these animals – they may have seen them in zoos or on wildlife programmes.
3. Read the introduction, drawing the student into the text so they will be keen to read the rest independently.

Module 9

Bart the champ

Follow the timetable on p.55. Use pp.29–46 to teach the Speed Sounds lessons. The Module activities follow the same steps for every Module. These steps are outlined in the blueprint teaching notes (see pp.56–61). In addition to the blueprint teaching notes, some activities require Module-specific teaching notes, which are outlined below. Answers to some activities are also provided.

First Read

1. Story introduction:

> Bart thinks fast cars are wicked. When a big race is announced, he wants to take part more than anything. But Bart doesn't have a car and he can't afford one. What he does have is an old pram. Undiscouraged by this, Bart goes to a local scrapyard to get some parts to make his pram into a racing car. But how will his creation hold up in the race? Will his arch-enemy Mad Mark beat him to the finish line?

2. Introductory question: Have you ever entered a race or competition?

3–6. Follow the remaining steps on p.58.

❓ Questions to Talk About

Note: This activity is only for small-group teaching.

Fastest Finger	What sort of car did Bart really want? (Section 1)
Fastest Finger	What did he collect from the scrapyard to make his new car? (Section 2)
Have a Think	How do you think Bart felt when the man said, "That car will not get you far!"? (Section 3)
Read with Expression	How did Bart feel after seeing Mad Mark's car? (*competitive, determined, ambitious*) Read aloud Section 3, showing feeling in Bart's words.
Fastest Finger	What happened to two of the leading cars? (Sections 5 and 6)
Read with Expression	How did the Queen feel about Bart? (*proud, respectful, pleased*) Read aloud Sections 7 and 8, showing feeling in the Queen's speech.

Spelling – Green Words

The completed grids should look like this:

	'best friends'	number of sounds		'best friends'	number of sounds
smart	ar	4	garden	ar	5
across	ss	5	party	ar	4
March	ar ch	3	present	none	7
track	ck	4	splash	sh	5
start	ar	4	cheek	ch ee	3

root + ending	root	ending
showing	show	ing
passed	pass	ed

Hold a Sentence

Bart went to a snack bar and had a hot dog at the track.

Proofread – spelling and punctuation

The correct text is: *Bart went to the garden party. The Queen took his arm. "I got you a present," she said. "Let me show you."*

Anthology – further reading

This Module links to the following texts on pp.27–34 of Anthology 2.

Fast track facts!

1. Ask the student to turn to p.27 in their Anthology.
2. Introduce them to the text 'Fast track facts!'. Ask them to talk about car racing and why people enjoy it, e.g. the excitement, speed, danger, drama, champion drivers, famous teams, cutting edge technology, etc.
3. Read the introduction, drawing the student into the text so they will be keen to read the rest independently.

Speed, skids and mud!

1. Ask the student to turn to p.32 in their Anthology.
2. Introduce them to the text 'Speed, skids and mud!'. Ask them to talk about what sort of challenges rally drivers might face, e.g. different sorts of road, night driving, extreme weather.
3. Read the first panel, drawing the student into the text so they will be keen to read the rest independently.

Module 10

Lorna

Follow the timetable on p.55. Use pp.29–46 to teach the Speed Sounds lessons. The Module activities follow the same steps for every Module. These steps are outlined in the blueprint teaching notes (see pp.56–61). In addition to the blueprint teaching notes, some activities require Module-specific teaching notes, which are outlined below. Answers to some activities are also provided.

First Read

1. Story introduction:

> Do you know anyone who had to start a new school? Do you know anyone who has been bullied? In this story, a girl called Lorna starts her new school and isn't getting on very well. Apart from Ella, Lorna doesn't know anyone. To make matters worse, the school bullies, Kelly and Zara, are making her life a misery. Until the school disco that is, when Josh Ford makes Lorna's day a little brighter.

2. Introductory question: How do you think you should respond to bullies? What should you say to them?

3–6. Follow the remaining steps on p.58.

Questions to Talk About

Note: This activity is only for small-group teaching.

Read with Expression	How did Kelly treat Lorna? (*She was bullying, mean, arrogant, cruel, unkind.*) Ask the student to read Section 2 aloud, using a suitable voice to express Kelly's attitude.
Fastest Finger	What did Kelly do to Lorna in the second bullying incident? (Section 3)
Fastest Finger	What did Lorna think about going to the disco? (Section 4)
Read with Expression	What do you think Josh felt about Kelly's bullying? (*disgusted, disappointed, angry, cross*) Ask the student to read Section 6 aloud, using an appropriate tone to show Josh's feelings.
Have a Think	How do you think Lorna felt about going to the disco with Josh? (Section 6)

Module 10

Spelling – Green Words

The completed grids should look like this:

	'best friends'	number of sounds		'best friends'	number of sounds
tore	ore	2	sch ool	ch oo	4
floor	oor	3	aff ord	ff or	4
sport	or	4	forty	or	4
story	or	4	morning	or ng	5
sh orts	sh or	4	before	ore	4

root + ending	root	ending
bored	bore	ed
grabbed	grab	ed
ignoring	ignore	ing
ignored	ignore	ed

Hold a Sentence

I was just finishing a story for English when Kelly tore it up.

Proofread – spelling and punctuation

The correct text is: *One night a disco was put on in the school hall. Ella said she'd meet me in the hall, so I went. Kelly and Zara were standing next to the door.*

A Anthology – further reading

This Module links to the following texts on pp.35–43 of Anthology 2.

Stay cool in school!

1. Ask the student to turn to p.35 in their Anthology.
2. Introduce them to the text 'Stay cool in school!'. Ask them what sort of attitudes and actions make some students appear 'cool'.
3. Read the introduction, drawing the student into the text so they will be keen to read the rest independently.

Which school is for you?

1. Ask the student to turn to p.39 in their Anthology.
2. Introduce them to the text 'Which school is for you?'. Ask them what they think would be their ideal school.
3. Read the first page, drawing the student into the text so they will be keen to read the rest independently.

Module 11

A bad hair day

Follow the timetable on p.55. Use pp.29–46 to teach the Speed Sounds lessons. The Module activities follow the same steps for every Module. These steps are outlined in the blueprint teaching notes (see pp.56–61). In addition to the blueprint teaching notes, some activities require Module-specific teaching notes, which are outlined below. Answers to some activities are also provided.

First Read

1. Story introduction:

> Today, we are going to read a story about a disaster with some hair dye. Fairways School has just broken up for the summer holidays. Best friends Ella and Willow are pleased to be out of school, and especially away from an annoying boy in their class, called Jack Haddow. Willow, who has always fancied herself as a hairdresser, offers to give Ella a new hairstyle. She invites Ella to her flat, and confidently begins to apply a bowl of maroon goo to her hair. What happens when Ella's new hair is revealed? Maybe the best friends could put the maroon goo to better use.

2. Introductory question: Have you ever tried something new because you were bored?

3–6. Follow the remaining steps on p.58.

Questions to Talk About

Note: This activity is only for small-group teaching.

Have a Think	How did Ella and Willow feel about the start of the holiday? (Section 1)
Have a Think	How did Willow convince Ella that things would be OK? (Section 3)
Have a Think	What mistake did Willow make? (Section 5)
Have a Think	What did Willow think about Ella's hair? (Section 6)
Read with Expression	How did Ella feel about her hair? (*appalled, shocked, upset, cross*) Read aloud her words in Section 6, showing her feelings.
Read with Expression	What sort of person is Willow's mother? (*practical, sensible*) Read aloud her words in Section 6, showing her personality and feelings.

Module 11

Spelling – Green Words

The completed grids should look like this:

	'best friends'	number of sounds		'best friends'	number of sounds
chair	ch air	2	flair	air	3
shampoo	sh oo	5	bright	igh	4
green	ee	4	Willow	ll ow	4
remark	ar	5	instruct	none	8

root + ending	root	ending
boring	bore	ing
grabbing	grab	ing

Hold a Sentence

Willow started to rub at a blob of goo that was stuck on the hairbrush.

Proofread – spelling and punctuation

The correct text is: *"Sit on this chair," instructed Willow. She started to mix up a bowl of maroon goo. "Will you be putting that stuff on my hair?" gasped Ella.*

A Anthology – further reading

This Module links to the following texts on pp.2–9 of Anthology 3.

Lairy hair

1. Ask the student to turn to p.2 in their Anthology.
2. Introduce them to the text 'Lairy hair'. Explain that this is a text full of fun hair-based facts!
3. Read the first page, drawing the student into the text so they will be keen to read the rest independently.

Mrs Fairborn's baby

1. Ask the student to turn to p.6 in their Anthology.
2. Introduce them to the text 'Mrs Fairborn's baby'. Explain that this text is a fairy tale based in a hair salon.
3. Read the first page, drawing the student into the text so they will be keen to read the rest independently.

Module 12

A good win for the red shirts

Follow the timetable on p.55. Use pp.29–46 to teach the Speed Sounds lessons. The Module activities follow the same steps for every Module. These steps are outlined in the blueprint teaching notes (see pp.56–61). In addition to the blueprint teaching notes, some activities require Module-specific teaching notes, which are outlined below. Answers to some activities are also provided.

First Read

1. Story introduction:

> Jonny Bird is the *Weekly Post's* top sports reporter. This week, he's reporting on a match between Manston United (Man U) and West Hampton at Hirst Park. West Hampton (in maroon shirts) start off strong, until Man U (in red shirts) come back fighting when their best player, Fred Irwin (who scored a hat-trick in their last match!) shows his flair.

2. Introductory question: Have you ever watched or played in a live sports match?

3–6. Follow the remaining steps on p.58.

? Questions to Talk About

Note: This activity is only for small-group teaching.

Fastest Finger	What match was Jonny Bird reporting on? (Section 1)
Fastest Finger	What was West Hampton's first tactic? Why did this not work at first? (Section 3)
Have a Think	Why was Boon described as a whirlwind? (Section 3)
Have a Think	Why did two girls run on to the pitch? (Section 5)
Fastest Finger	Who scored the final goal and won the match? (Section 6)
Read with Expression	What does the reporter want his readers to feel in Section 7? (*excited, uplifted, happy*) Read aloud Section 7, showing these feelings.

Spelling – Green Words

The completed grids should look like this:

	'best friends'	number of sounds		'best friends'	number of sounds
th irty	th ir	4	bir thday	ir th ay	5
sight	igh	3	dirty	ir	4
th irteen	th ir ee	5	match	tch	3
sport	or	4	th irsty	th ir	5
girl	ir	3	sh irt	sh ir	3

root + ending	root	ending
resulted	result	ed
scoring	score	ing
stirred	stir	ed

Hold a Sentence

Feelings ran high and the fans swirled flags in the air.

Proofread – spelling and punctuation

The correct text is: *The third scoring ball of the match was shot in by Irwin. This was his second winning shot. It resulted from a quick throw-in and then a good pass from the left.*

A | Anthology – further reading

This Module links to the following texts on pp.10–17 of Anthology 3.

What sort of football fan are you?

1. Ask the student to turn to p.10 in their Anthology.
2. Introduce them to the text 'What sort of football fan are you – fanatical, fair or a flop?'. Explain that this is a fun quiz to find out how much they know about football. There are six questions and they have to choose an answer from a, b or c. Then they tot up their scores and find out what sort of fan they are on the final page.
3. Read the introduction and the first question aloud. Encourage the student to read the rest of the text in their own time.

It's football – but not as we know it!

1. Ask the student to turn to p.14 in their Anthology.
2. Introduce them to the text 'It's football – but not as we know it!'. Explain that this is a text about how football used to be played. Ensure they understand that the text goes on to look at some of the old football rules (in light brown panels on the next pages). Point out that the pictures show what some of the old football matches might have looked like!
3. Read the first page, drawing the student into the text so they will be keen to read the rest independently.

Module 13

A player to be proud of

Follow the timetable on p.55. Use pp.29–46 to teach the Speed Sounds lessons. The Module activities follow the same steps for every Module. These steps are outlined in the blueprint teaching notes (see pp.56–61). In addition to the blueprint teaching notes, some activities require Module-specific teaching notes, which are outlined below. Answers to some activities are also provided.

First Read

1. Story introduction:

> Have you ever heard of David Beckham? David Beckham is a famous footballer. He was born to an ordinary family in London and rose to super-stardom as England's skipper. This is a short biography of him. It provides information about the most important events of his life and his family, Victoria, Brooklyn, Romeo, Cruz, Harper.

2. Introductory question: Who is your favourite sportsman or sportswoman, and why?

3–6. Follow the remaining steps on p.58.

? Questions to Talk About

Note: This activity is only for small-group teaching.

Fastest Finger	Where was David born? (Section 1)
Fastest Finger	Which sections tell us that David had very early success? (Sections 4 and 5)
Have a Think	What were the highest points in his career? (Section 6)
Have a Think	What were the lowest points in his career? (Section 7)
Fastest Finger	Who is David married to and what are the names of his children? (Sections 8, 10, 12)
Read with Expression	What does the author of this biography feel about David Beckham? (*proud, impressed, in awe, envious, respectful*) Read Section 13 aloud, showing the feelings of the author.

Spelling – Green Words

The completed grids should look like this:

	'best friends'	number of sounds		'best friends'	number of sounds
proud	ou	4	around	ou	5
bench	ch	4	charity	ch	6
ground	ou	5	penalty	none	7
count	ou	4	kitchen	tch	5
sh out	sh ou	3	amount	ou	5

root + ending	root	ending
kicking	kick	ing
slouches	slouch	es

Hold a Sentence

David slouches off and England must play with just ten men.

Proofread – spelling and punctuation

The correct text is: *His mum Sandra is a hairdresser. His dad Ted is a kitchen fitter. David is a lad who loves football. He is always kicking or bouncing a ball.*

A Anthology – further reading

This Module links to the following texts on pp.18–25 of Anthology 3.

Norman Knight, time-travelling superstar

1. Ask the student to turn to p.18 in their Anthology.
2. Introduce them to the text 'Norman Knight, time-travelling superstar'. Explain that this story is told by two sports commentators watching a football match. It is about a time-travelling footballer who arrives to play in an FA Cup semi-final.
3. Read the introduction, drawing the student into the text so they will be keen to read the rest independently.

Christmas 1914

1. Ask the student to turn to p.22 in their Anthology.
2. Introduce them to the text 'Christmas 1914'. Explain that the text is based on actual events during the First World War.
3. Read the first panel, drawing the student into the text so they will be keen to read the rest independently.

Module 14

Cook – and enjoy!

Follow the timetable on p.55. Use pp.29–46 to teach the Speed Sounds lessons. The Module activities follow the same steps for every Module. These steps are outlined in the blueprint teaching notes (see pp.56–61). In addition to the blueprint teaching notes, some activities require Module-specific teaching notes, which are outlined below. Answers to some activities are also provided.

First Read

1. Story introduction:

> Do you enjoy cooking? What sort of things do you like to make? Have you ever made pancakes? This is a recipe for yummy lemony pancakes. Read how to make the perfect pancake, but remember – never cook without an adult to help you!

2. Introductory question: What is your favourite food?

3–6. Follow the remaining steps on p.58.

? Questions to Talk About

Note: This activity is only for small-group teaching.

Fastest Finger	Which are the runny ingredients? ('You will need' section)
Fastest Finger	Which are the dry ingredients? ('You will need' section)
Have a Think	At which part or parts of the recipe would you need to help a young child? (Sections 2, 6, 7, 8, 9)
Have a Think	Pick out the verbs which tell you what to do; they are known as imperative verbs and they give instructions. (*try, mix, lift, scoop, whisk, add, tip, put, swirl, cook, drop, flip, lay, stack, squeeze, sweeten, enjoy*) (All sections)
Read with Expression	If you were the cook writing this recipe, how would you imagine saying the final word 'enjoy'? (*with a smile, with enthusiasm, with warmth, with good humour*) Read Section 10 aloud, putting lots of feeling in the final word.

Spelling – Green Words

The completed grids should look like this:

	'best friends'	number of sounds		'best friends'	number of sounds
point	oi	4	scor ch	or ch	4
spoil	oi	4	firm	ir	3
foil	oi	3	smoo th	oo th	4
fresh	sh	4	enjoy	oy	4
light	igh	3	avoid	oi	4
whisk	wh	4	electric	none	8

root + ending	root	ending
spoiled	spoil	ed
annoyed	annoy	ed
boiling	boil	ing

Hold a Sentence

Put the pan on the ring and swirl the oil around as it gets hot.

Proofread – spelling and punctuation

The correct text is: *To keep the pancakes hot as you cook more, lay a flat dish on top of a pan of boiling water and stack the pancakes on the dish. Put a sheet of foil on top.*

A Anthology – further reading

This Module links to the following texts on pp.26–33 of Anthology 3.

Troy Tomato cooks up a storm

1. Ask the student to turn to p.26 in their Anthology.
2. Introduce them to the text 'Troy Tomato cooks up a storm'. Explain that this is an interview with a TV chef while he demonstrates his cooking 'skills'. Point out that the interviewer is called 'Joy' and the chef is 'Troy'.
3. Read the introduction, drawing the student into the text so they will be keen to read the rest independently.

Unwrap – and enjoy!

1. Ask the student to turn to p.30 in their Anthology.
2. Introduce them to the text 'Unwrap – and enjoy!'. Explain that this text tells the history of chocolate, how chocolates and chocolate bars are made and interesting facts about chocolate.
3. Read the first page, drawing the student into the text so they will be keen to read the rest independently.

Module 15

Late

Follow the timetable on p.55. Use pp.29–46 to teach the Speed Sounds lessons. The Module activities follow the same steps for every Module. These steps are outlined in the blueprint teaching notes (see pp.56–61). In addition to the blueprint teaching notes, some activities require Module-specific teaching notes, which are outlined below. Answers to some activities are also provided.

First Read

1. Story introduction:

> Have you ever been late for something important? The boy in this story-poem is late for school. He explains to his teacher, Miss Tate, why he is so late but uses excuses instead of telling the truth. After telling Miss Tate a string of crazy stories involving snakes, cakes, balls, walls, the moon and balloons, he finally admits what *really* happened that morning.

2. Introductory question: Have you ever made up an excuse for being late?

3–6. Follow the remaining steps on p.58.

Questions to Talk About

Note: This activity is only for small-group teaching.

Fastest Finger	List the main excuses, briefly (e.g. *had to look for mate's snake, had to go to the shop, kicked a ball that smashed a window, trip to the moon, octopus thief, played with cat, dog ate lunch, food fight*).
Have a Think	Which do you think is the most unbelievable excuse and why?
Read with Expression	How do you think the boy feels about being late? (*sorry, apologetic, worried, lighthearted*) Read Section 1 with expression, showing the boy's feelings.
Have a Think	How do you think Miss Tate might have felt when she listened to these excuses? (*exasperated, cross, annoyed, amused*) What might she have said at the end?
Read with Expression	How do you think his mate's mum felt when she found the boys in a food fight? (*furious, annoyed, shocked, angry*) Read the last paragraph in Section 7, showing her feelings.

Module 15

Spelling – Green Words

The completed grids should look like this:

	'best friends'	number of sounds		'best friends'	number of sounds
snake	a-e	4	make	a-e	3
late	a-e	3	hate	a-e	3
rage	a-e	3	marmalade	ar a-e	7
more	ore	2	fate	a-e	3
made	a-e	3	chocolate	ch a-e	7

root + ending	root	ending
baked	bake	ed
hated	hate	ed
escaped	escape	ed

Hold a Sentence

My mate has a snake that got in a rage and bit him.

Proofread – spelling and punctuation

The correct text is: Then <u>I</u> chucked a tomato in my mate<u>'</u>s fa<u>ce</u>, so he bashed me with his pen<u>c</u>il case<u>.</u> Then we grab<u>b</u>ed lots of food and had a good fight.

> **A** **Anthology – further reading**
>
> This Module links to the following texts on pp.34–43 of Anthology 3.
>
> **Room rage!**
> 1. Ask the student to turn to p.34 in their Anthology.
> 2. Introduce them to the text 'Room rage!'. Ensure they understand the concept of 'room rage', i.e. when an adult gets worked up about the state of your bedroom.
> 3. Read the introduction, drawing the student into the text so they will be keen to read the rest independently.
>
> **Get your skates on!**
> 1. Ask the student to turn to p.39 in their Anthology.
> 2. Introduce them to the text 'Get your skates on!'. Explain that 'Get your skates on' can mean 'hurry up'.
> 3. Read the first page with the student. Suggest that they read aloud Jake's words, while you read aloud Mum and Miss Tate's words. Be sure to draw the student into the text so they will be keen to read the rest independently.

Module 16

The weaving contest

Follow the timetable on p.55. Use pp.29–46 to teach the Speed Sounds lessons. The Module activities follow the same steps for every Module. These steps are outlined in the blueprint teaching notes (see pp.56–61). In addition to the blueprint teaching notes, some activities require Module-specific teaching notes, which are outlined below. Answers to some activities are also provided.

First Read

1. Story introduction:

> This story is set in Ancient Greece. The two main characters are called Athene (pronounced *ath-ee-nee*) and Arachne (pronounced *a-rack-nee*). Athene is a Greek goddess who is famous for weaving beautiful, exquisite tapestries. But one day she receives a shock. She hears that a human called Arachne is 'stealing her thunder', boasting that she can weave the most beautiful tapestries in the world. The goddess Athene is so angry that she challenges Arachne to a weaving contest. However, she is shocked when she sees that Arachne's tapestries really are more beautiful than hers. Her jealousy leads her to wreak the most horrible revenge upon Arachne.

2. Introductory question: When have you felt jealous of someone else?

3–6. Follow the remaining steps on p.58.

⁇ Questions to Talk About

Note: This activity is only for small-group teaching.

Fastest Finger	Why is the goddess Athene shocked? (Section 1)
Have a Think	How do we know that Athene is competitive? (Section 3)
Fastest Finger	Describe Arachne's tapestry. (Sections 6 and 7)
Read with Expression	How does Athene feel when she sees Arachne's tapestry? (*Disbelief, then admiration, then anger*.) Read her words in Section 7, showing her feelings.
Have a Think	How do you think Arachne feels when the spell is cast? (If necessary, draw out the fact she has been turned into a spider.) (Section 8)

Spelling – Green Words

The completed grids should look like this:

	'best friends'	number of sounds		'best friends'	number of sounds
name	a-e	3	teach	ea ch	3
take	a-e	3	scream	ea	5
girl	ir	3	cheat	ch ea	3
know	kn ow	2	beautiful	ea	8
face	a-e	3	real	ea	3
dream	ea	4	fantastic	none	9

root + ending	root	ending
creaked	creak	ed
screamed	scream	ed
seated	seat	ed

Hold a Sentence

I will pick you up and hang you from the beam.

Proofread – spelling and punctuation

The correct text is: *Our arms move back and forth across the bright cloth. The looms are creaking. As we weave, no one speaks. I know my tapestry will be the best.*

Anthology – further reading

This Module links to the following texts on pp.2–9 of Anthology 4.

Peacocks or peanuts – Dr Dean looks at strange phobias

1. Ask the student to turn to p.2 in their Anthology.
2. Introduce them to the text 'Peacocks or peanuts – Dr Dean looks at strange phobias'. Explain that this is a text about people's phobias.
3. Read the first page, drawing the student into the text so they will be keen to read the rest independently.

Monsters of land, air and sea

1. Ask the student to turn to p.6 in their Anthology.
2. Introduce them to the text 'Monsters of land, air and sea'. Explain that this is a text about mythical Greek creatures. You may need to explain how to say the names of the characters: Sirens (*sigh-rens*), Cyclops (*sigh-clops*), Zeus (*z-you-s*), Odysseus (*o-dee-see-us*), Scylla (*silla*), Minotaur (*mine-o-tor*), Satyrs (*sat-ers*), Gorgons (*gor-gons*), Sphinx (*s-f-inx*)
3. Read the first page, drawing the student into the text so they will be keen to read the rest independently.

Module 17

Amy Oliver's quick goldfish pie

Follow the timetable on p.55. Use pp.29–46 to teach the Speed Sounds lessons. The Module activities follow the same steps for every Module. These steps are outlined in the blueprint teaching notes (see pp.56–61). In addition to the blueprint teaching notes, some activities require Module-specific teaching notes, which are outlined below. Answers to some activities are also provided.

First Read

1. Story introduction:

> Today, we are going to read a recipe. You may have heard of the TV chef Jamie Oliver, but have you heard of Amy Oliver? They're not related, but Amy also writes fantastic, if a little strange, recipes. You might be a little surprised by her style! Can you spot what might be different in Amy's recipe compared to a usual one?

2. Introductory question: What did you make the last time you followed a recipe?

3–6. Follow the remaining steps on p.58.

Questions to Talk About

Note: This activity is only for small-group teaching.

Fastest Finger	What are the two subheadings in this recipe? (Sections 1 and 3)
Fastest Finger	Pick out the imperative verbs (instruction words) in Section 6 (*bake, allow, divide, garnish, add, open, take*).
Have a Think	In what ways does this recipe seem normal? (Examples could be selected from all sections, e.g. *the numbering, the tips and advice*.)
Have a Think	Which is your favourite part of this recipe, and why?
Read with Expression	Most recipes are serious in tone. Read out one section of this recipe in a suitable tone.

Spelling – Green Words

The completed grids should look like this:

	'best friends'	number of sounds		'best friends'	number of sounds
good	oo	3	time	i-e	3
leave	ea ve	3	smile	i-e	4
taste	a-e	4	quite	qu i-e	3
bake	a-e	3	meanwhile	ea wh i-e	6
first	ir	4	divide	i-e	5
nice	i-e	3	decorate	or a-e	6
while	wh i-e	3	advice	i-e	5

root + ending	root	ending
slicing	slice	ing
wiping	wipe	ing
biting	bite	ing

Hold a Sentence

First, catch your potato, dice it and freeze it.

Proofread – spelling and punctuation

The correct text is: *With a sharp knife, slice the boiled ice cream into neat slices and line the pie dish with them. (Ask an adult to help you with this bit.)*

Anthology – further reading

This Module links to the following texts on pp.10–17 of Anthology 4.

Down the hatch!

1. Ask the student to turn to p.10 in their Anthology.
2. Introduce them to the text 'Down the hatch!'. Explain that this is a text about horrible foods.
3. Read the first page, drawing the student into the text so they will be keen to read the rest independently.

Wild Mike's guide to staying alive!

1. Ask the student to turn to p.14 in their Anthology.
2. Introduce them to the text 'Wild Mike's guide to staying alive!'. Explain that this is a text about dangerous animals.
3. Read the first page, drawing the student into the text so they will be keen to read the rest independently.

Module 18

Beep!

Follow the timetable on p.55. Use pp.29–46 to teach the Speed Sounds lessons. The Module activities follow the same steps for every Module. These steps are outlined in the blueprint teaching notes (see pp.56–61). In addition to the blueprint teaching notes, some activities require Module-specific teaching notes, which are outlined below. Answers to some activities are also provided.

First Read

1. Story introduction:

> Have you ever heard the phrase 'Be careful what you wish for'? In this story, Jack Cope is jealous of his friend Gopal's mobile phone. He starts off thinking Gopal is a bit silly for having one, but soon wants one himself. After coming to an agreement with his grandad (which involves cleaning his van for six weeks!), Jack gets his wish. However, he soon find out that having a mobile phone is not all it's cracked up to be.

2. Introductory question: What is the last thing you begged your parents for? Were you successful?

3–6. Follow the remaining steps on p.58.

Questions to Talk About

Note: This activity is only for small-group teaching.

Have a Think	What did Jack think about mobile phones and their users at the start of the story? (Section 1)
Fastest Finger	Who did Gopal text and why? (Section 2)
Have a Think	Why did Jack's mum say he couldn't have a phone? (Sections 5 and 6)
Fastest Finger	How did Jack buy his new phone? (Section 7)
Read with Expression	How did Mum feel about the phone once Jack had one? (*she liked it, was enthusiastic, wanted to make use of it*) Read aloud Section 9, saying Mum's words with suitable feeling.
Read with Expression	Was Jack pleased with his new phone? (*He was fed up/annoyed with his mum calling him, asking him to do things. He was more interested in Gopal's new tablet.*) Read Section 10 aloud, showing Jack's feelings towards the phone and Gopal's new tablet.

Module 18

Spelling – Green Words

The completed grids should look like this:

	'best friends'	number of sounds		'best friends'	number of sounds
mine	i-e	3	spoke	o-e	4
late	a-e	3	cajole	o-e	5
like	i-e	3	ringtone	ng o-e	6
phone	ph o-e	3	forgotten	or tt	7
home	o-e	3	alone	o-e	4

root + ending	root	ending
joking	joke	ing
hoping	hope	ing
closing	close	ing

Hold a Sentence

Jack picked up his bike and rode home alone.

Proofread – spelling and punctuation

The correct text is: *Mum almost choked on her tea. "You must be joking! Do you know what those things cost? Mobile phones are always getting stolen!"*

A | Anthology – further reading

This Module links to the following texts on pp.18–27 of Anthology 4.

The phone zone

1. Ask the student to turn to p.18 in their Anthology.
2. Introduce them to the text 'The phone zone'. Ask them to talk about what they like or dislike about mobile phones, and why.
3. Read the introduction, drawing the student into the text so they will be keen to read the rest independently.

Home-grown sound effect zone!

1. Ask the student to turn to p.24 in their Anthology.
2. Introduce them to the text 'Home-grown sound effect zone!'. Explain that this text looks at how to make your own sound effects for a school play or radio programme.
3. Read the first page, drawing the student into the text so they will be keen to read the rest independently.

Module 19

Spellbound

Follow the timetable on p.55. Use pp.29–46 to teach the Speed Sounds lessons. The Module activities follow the same steps for every Module. These steps are outlined in the blueprint teaching notes (see pp.56–61). In addition to the blueprint teaching notes, some activities require Module-specific teaching notes, which are outlined below. Answers to some activities are also provided.

First Read

1. Story introduction:

> Princess Janet is bored. Her dad, the king, is often away hunting, shooting and fishing, meaning Janet is left alone in the castle to amuse herself. One day Janet leaves the castle and heads to the forest to pick bluebells. There she meets Tam Lin, an Elfin Knight who is under the spell of the queen of witches. On Halloween, Janet finds out that Tam Lin is not all he seems. But she does leave the forest with more than just bluebells.

2. Introductory question: Have you ever been trick or treating on Halloween? What did you dress up as?

3–6. Follow the remaining steps on p.58.

Questions to Talk About

Note: This activity is only for small-group teaching.

Have a Think	Why did Janet think that the 'dude' was confused? (Sections 2 and 3)
Read with Expression	How does Janet feel about the 'dude's' first words? (*She is cross/furious with him because he seems rude and has no right to tell her what to do.*) Read Janet's words aloud with expression, showing her feelings towards the 'dude'. (Section 3)
Fastest Finger	What was the Elfin Knight's story? (Section 5)
Read with Expression	How did Janet feel as she watched the queen of the witches and the goblins pass by? (*thrilled, excited, impressed, amused*) Read aloud Section 7, showing her feelings.
Fastest Finger	What happened when Janet dragged Tam Lin from his horse? (Sections 8 and 9)
Have a Think	Was it a happy-ever-after ending? (Section 9)

Spelling – Green Words

The completed grids should look like this:

	'best friends'	number of sounds		'best friends'	number of sounds
kn ow	kn ow	2	rule	u-e	3
name	a-e	3	blue	ue	3
true	ue	3	huge	u-e	3
brick	ck	4	confuse	u-e	6
hide	i-e	3	refuse	u-e	5
tune	u-e	3	amuse	u-e	4

root + ending	root	ending
confusing	confuse	ing
refusing	refuse	ing
amusing	amuse	ing
consumed	consume	ed

Hold a Sentence

First came the queen of the witches, sitting on a huge black horse.

Proofread – spelling and punctuation

The correct text is: *So, on Halloween, I got out of bed just before midnight and went to hide. Before long there was a huge noise. Horses' hooves, bells going like the clappers – the lot!*

> **A** **Anthology – further reading**
>
> This Module links to the following texts on pp.28–35 of Anthology 4.
>
> **Duke weds royal bride in wedding of the season!**
> 1. Ask the student to turn to p.28 in their Anthology.
> 2. Introduce them to the text 'Duke weds royal bride in wedding of the season!' Explain that it is a magazine article about a royal wedding.
> 3. Read the first page, drawing the student into the text so they will be keen to read the rest independently.
>
> **Happy ever after?**
> 1. Ask the student to turn to p.32 in their Anthology.
> 2. Introduce them to the text 'Happy ever after?'. Explain that it is a quiz about whether they will find their own fairy-tale ending. Read the introduction and the first question. Ask the student which of the three options describes what they would do – a, b or c. Tell them to note down the option they choose.
> 3. Encourage the student to do the rest of the quiz in their own time, totting up their scores at the end.

Module 20

The Outlaws

Follow the timetable on p.55. Use pp.29–46 to teach the Speed Sounds lessons. The Module activities follow the same steps for every Module. These steps are outlined in the blueprint teaching notes (see pp.56–61). In addition to the blueprint teaching notes, some activities require Module-specific teaching notes, which are outlined below. Answers to some activities are also provided.

First Read

1. Story introduction:

> The only problem with setting up a band with your mates is you have to put up with the instruments they play. The Grimshaw lads are in a band called the Outlaws. Sam plays the drums, Shaun plays the bass and Paul plays the bagpipes – badly! It's only when they perform at the Hawthorn Club that Sam and Shaun realise it isn't just them who can't stand Paul's caterwauling. Luckily, star vocalist Laura Lipgloss is in the audience.

2. Introductory question: Do you play a musical instrument? Would you like to be in a band?

3–6. Follow the remaining steps on p.58.

? Questions to Talk About

Note: This activity is only for small-group teaching.

Have a Think	What was the main problem with the band? (Section 2)
Have a Think	What did the audience think about the band at the start of the concert? (Section 3)
Fastest Finger	What was Sam's solution to the problem? (Section 5)
Read with Expression	How did Paul feel after he discovered the trick? (*furious, humiliated, angry, determined to quit*) How did Saul feel about the outcome? (*pleased, amused, positive*) Read aloud Section 6, showing the feelings of both Paul and Saul.
Have a Think	What did the audience think about the band after Laura Lipgloss had joined? (Section 6)

Spelling – Green Words

The completed grids should look like this:

	'best friends'	number of sounds		'best friends'	number of sounds
sing	ng	3	dawn	aw	3
awful	aw	4	sprawl	aw	5
yawn	aw	3	taunt	au	4
crawl	aw	4	applause	pp au se	5
Lipgloss	ss	7	audience	au ce	6

root + ending	root	ending
sprawled	sprawl	ed
yawned	yawn	ed
taunted	taunt	ed

Hold a Sentence

A burst of applause greeted The Outlaws as they took to the stage.

Proofread – spelling and punctuation

The correct text is: *"You filled the bagpipes with coke!"* groaned Paul as he crawled off the stage. *"Right, that's it! I've had it with the Outlaws."*

Anthology – further reading

This Module links to the following texts on pp.36–43 of Anthology 4.

Awesome!

1. Ask the student to turn to p.36 in their Anthology.
2. Introduce them to the text 'Awesome!' Explain that it is about being in a band. Ask them to talk about their favourite (or their own) band, briefly.
3. Read the introduction, drawing the student into the text so they will be keen to read the rest independently.

The Fab Factor

1. Ask the student to turn to p.39 in their Anthology.
2. Introduce them to the text 'The Fab Factor'. Explain that this text is about a talent show and is written as a playscript. Point out the characters' names and stage directions.
3. Read the first page, drawing the student into the text so they will be keen to read the rest independently.

Module 21

Romeo and Juliet

Follow the timetable on p.55. Use pp.29–46 to teach the Speed Sounds lessons. The Module activities follow the same steps for every Module. These steps are outlined in the blueprint teaching notes (see pp.56–61). In addition to the blueprint teaching notes, some activities require Module-specific teaching notes, which are outlined below. Answers to some activities are also provided.

First Read

1. Story introduction:

> This text is a summary of a play written by William Shakespeare. The play was written over four hundred years ago, and takes place in a city in Italy called Verona. The city is ruled by two feuding families – the Montagues (*mont-ag-yoos*) and the Capulets (*cap-you-lets*). The families have hated each other for many years and things are about to get more difficult. When Romeo (a Montague) and Juliet (a Capulet) accidently meet at a ball, they fall in love instantly. But this is just the beginning …

2. Introductory question: What do you know about William Shakespeare?

3–6. Follow the remaining steps on p.58.

Questions to Talk About

Note: This activity is only for small-group teaching.

Fastest Finger	What was Romeo and Juliet's first problem? (Sections 1, 2, 3, 4)
Have a Think	What events made the problem even worse? (Sections 6 and 8)
Fastest Finger	What solution did the monk have to solve their problem? (Section 9)
Fastest Finger	Why did this solution fail to work? (Sections 10, 11, 12, 13, 14)
Read with Expression	This story is a tragedy, which means it has an unhappy ending. How do you think the families felt about the outcome? (*sad, distraught, heartbroken*) Read aloud Sections 13 and 14 in a suitable voice, showing the tragedy of the events.

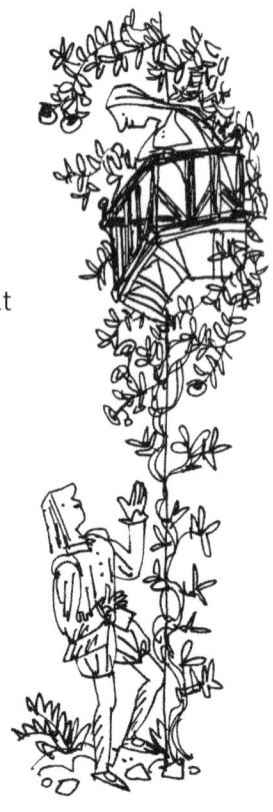

Module 21

Spelling – Green Words

The completed grids should look like this:

	'best friends'	number of sounds		'best friends'	number of sounds
fair	air	2	compare	are	5
share	sh are	2	beware	are	4
care	are	2	farewell	are ll	5
spare	are	3	unaware	are	5

root + ending	root	ending
glaring	glare	ing
glared	glare	ed
preparing	prepare	ing
sharing	share	ing

Hold a Sentence

In the soft light of the flare, he saw a girl who was as fair as the sun.

Proofread – spelling and punctuation

The correct text is: Romeo arrived at the tomb at midnight, but Paris was there, too. Paris tried to stop Romeo from opening the tomb, so Romeo killed him.

> **A** **Anthology – further reading**
>
> This Module links to the following texts on pp.2–10 of Anthology 5.
>
> **A fanfare for Monio and Oojilet**
>
> 1. Ask the student to turn to p.2 in their Anthology.
> 2. Introduce them to the text 'A fanfare for Monio and Oojilet'. Explain that this is a fun retelling of the Romeo and Juliet story in the modern day.
> 3. Read the first page, drawing the student into the text so they will be keen to read the rest independently.
>
> **Once upon a love match**
>
> 1. Ask the student to turn to p.7 in their Anthology.
> 2. Introduce them to the text 'Once upon a love match'. Explain that this text is taken from a dating website for fairy-tale characters.
> 3. Read the first page, drawing the student into the text so they will be keen to read the rest independently.

Module 22

Sunburst Teen Magazine

Follow the timetable on p.55. Use pp.29–46 to teach the Speed Sounds lessons. The Module activities follow the same steps for every Module. These steps are outlined in the blueprint teaching notes (see pp.56–61). In addition to the blueprint teaching notes, some activities require Module-specific teaching notes, which are outlined below. Answers to some activities are also provided.

First Read

1. Story introduction:

> Do you know what a 'problem page' is? It's a page in a magazine which has letters written by people who want advice. Some people find it difficult to talk to other people about their problems – they may feel embarrassed or think people will treat them differently once they have told them, so they write to a problem page asking for help. Arthur, an expert at the magazine, tries to help find a solution to the problems and answers the letters. This text is an example of a problem page.

2. Introductory question: Would you ever write in to a problem page? Why or why not?

3–6. Follow the remaining steps on p.58.

? Questions to Talk About

Note: This activity is only for small-group teaching.

Fastest Finger	What do the bullies do to KG? (Section 1)
Read with Expression	How do you think IP feels? (*lonely, sad, unhappy, hurt*) Read aloud Section 3, with feeling.
Have a Think	What would you advise IP to do? (Section 3)
Read with Expression	What sort of attitude does Arthur have? (*firm, decisive, encouraging, positive, strong*) Read aloud Section 4, with feeling.
Have a Think	What would you advise JMcT to do? (Section 4)

Spelling – Green Words

The completed grids should look like this:

	'best friends'	number of sounds		'best friends'	number of sounds
purple	ur le	4	ch urn	ch ur	3
blurt	ur	4	fur th er	ur th er	4
burst	ur	4	tea ch er	ea ch er	4
curly	ur	4	remember	er	7
turn	ur	3	advice	i-e	5

root + ending	root	ending
pleased	please	ed
blurted	blurt	ed

Hold a Sentence

They tease me about my curly hair and lurk outside the shops waiting for me.

Proofread – spelling and punctuation

The correct text is: *There was a five-pound note in it. She just blurted it out to me one day, but I wish she hadn't told me. Do I tell the teacher or do I stay loyal to the girl?*

Anthology – further reading

This Module links to the following texts on pp.11–19 of Anthology 5.

Ask Shirley …

1. Ask the student to turn to p.11 in their Anthology.
2. Introduce them to the text 'Ask Shirley …'. Explain that it is another problem page in a magazine.
3. Read the introduction to the student and the first letter, from Irma. Ask them how they think Shirley should respond. Encourage the student to read the rest of the text independently.

Many happy returns Sunburst!

1. Ask the student to turn to p.15 in their Anthology.
2. Introduce them to the text 'Many happy returns Sunburst!'. Explain that this text is a birthday special of the *Sunburst* teen magazine.
3. Read the first page, drawing the student into the text so they will be keen to read the rest independently.

Module 23

How does it feel to be an astronaut?

Follow the timetable on p.55. Use pp.29–46 to teach the Speed Sounds lessons. The Module activities follow the same steps for every Module. These steps are outlined in the blueprint teaching notes (see pp.56–61). In addition to the blueprint teaching notes, some activities require Module-specific teaching notes, which are outlined below. Answers to some activities are also provided.

First Read

1. Story introduction:

> Have you ever heard of Major Tim Peake? Tim Peake is a British astronaut who spent six months on the International Space Station. While he was in space, he did experiments on the environment and tested out new technologies for future missions. So what is it like to be an astronaut? How must it feel when the hatch is closed and the engines ignite, ready to take you thousands of miles into space? This text is an interview with a fictional astronaut who answers some of these questions.

2. Introductory question: Would you like to go into space? Why or why not?

3–6. Follow the remaining steps on p.58.

Questions to Talk About

Note: This activity is only for small-group teaching.

Have a Think	What does it mean when it says 'prepare yourself mentally for the flight'? (Section 1)
Have a Think	Why does the rocket go faster as the fuel is used up? (Section 3)
Fastest Finger	In what way do astronauts look like clowns? (Section 4)
Fastest Finger	Why do astronauts like salt and pepper on their food? (Section 7)
Have a Think	Why are drinks taken from a squeeze bottle? (Section 7)
Fastest Finger	What do astronauts enjoy most? (Section 8)
Fastest Finger	Why is it rare for an astronaut to be ill in space? (Section 9)

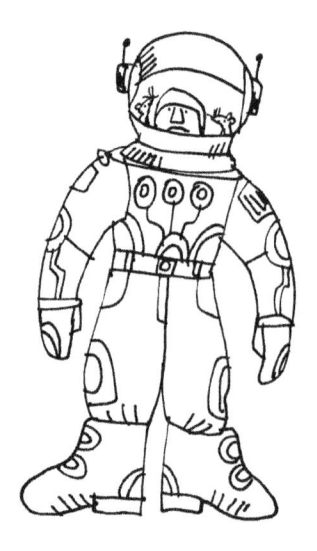

Module 23

Spelling – Green Words

The completed grids should look like this:

	'best friends'	number of sounds		'best friends'	number of sounds
squ ee ze	qu ee ze	4	liquid	qu	5
crowd	ow	4	brea the	ea the	4
surr ound	rr ou	6	ground	ou	5
medical	none	7	message	ss a-e	5
becau se	au se	5	terrific	rr	7

root + ending	root	ending
bumpier	bumpy	er
easier	easy	er

Hold a Sentence

The checks were complete so the rocket could be launched.

Proofread – spelling and punctuation

The correct text is: *How do astronauts spend their spare time? Some read, or watch films, or write messages home on their laptops. Most astronauts also enjoy watching earth from the windows.*

A Anthology – further reading

This Module links to the following texts on pp.20–26 of Anthology 5.

A spell in space

1. Ask the student to turn to p.20 in their Anthology.
2. Introduce them to the text 'A spell in space'. Explain that it is a poem about an astronaut in space. Ask the student to talk about two of the different meanings of the word 'spell'. (It can mean something magical, or it can mean a short time.) Tell the student that this poem uses this word in both ways.
3. Read the first panel, drawing the student into the text so they will be keen to read the rest independently.

They came from outer space!

1. Ask the student to turn to p.23 in their Anthology.
2. Introduce them to the text 'They came from outer space!'. Explain that this text is all about whether or not life exists on other planets and includes accounts from people seeing unidentified flying objects.
3. Read the first panel, drawing the student into the text so they will be keen to read the rest independently.

Module 24

Game raider

Follow the timetable on p.55. Use pp.29–46 to teach the Speed Sounds lessons. The Module activities follow the same steps for every Module. These steps are outlined in the blueprint teaching notes (see pp.56–61). In addition to the blueprint teaching notes, some activities require Module-specific teaching notes, which are outlined below. Answers to some activities are also provided.

First Read

1. Story introduction:

> Sam Brown is a self-confessed gamer. 'Gamer' means someone who loves to play computer games, and spends most of their free time doing it! When Sam orders the latest game, 'Brain Raider', online he expects it to be with him the following week. When the order is delivered, Sam eagerly opens the box to find it is empty and the game is missing. He furiously emails the online company to complain. This text is the email conversation between Sam and Bob Brain from the company, Brainwave Games.

2. Introductory question: Have you ever complained about something? Did you get what you wanted?

3–6. Follow the remaining steps on p.58.

Questions to Talk About

Note: This activity is only for small-group teaching.

Fastest Finger	How did Sam order the computer game? (Section 1)
Have a Think	What was very silly about Bob's reply? (Section 2)
Have a Think	How did Sam make sure that Bob knew he was very annoyed? (Section 3)
Read with Expression	What does Sam feel when Bob asks him to wait a month or so before he sends the game? (*furious, exasperated, angry, outraged*) Read aloud Section 5, showing Sam's feelings.
Read with Expression	How do you think Bob feels about being in prison and his future? (*matter-of-fact, positive, optimistic*) Read aloud Section 6, showing Bob's feelings.

Spelling – Green Words

The completed grids should look like this:

	'best friends'	number of sounds		'best friends'	number of sounds
strain	ai	5	complain	ai	7
straight	aigh	5	contain	ai	6
eighteen	eigh ee	4	address	dd ss	5
write	wr i-e	3	mistake	a-e	6
quite	qu i-e	3	recent	none	6

root + ending	root	ending
useful	use	ful
useless	use	less
recently	recent	ly

Hold a Sentence

If you fail to return my payment, I will make your life very difficult indeed.

Proofread – spelling and punctuation

The correct text is: *My main problem is that these games are made in Spain, and the stock does not always arrive as quickly as I would like. In fact I have been under lots of strain recently and the doctor says it's all because of my stressful job.*

> **A** **Anthology – further reading**
>
> This Module links to the following texts on pp.27–34 of Anthology 5.
>
> **Do it!**
> 1. Ask the student to turn to p.27 in their Anthology.
> 2. Introduce them to the text 'Do it!'. Explain that this text is full of ideas for activities to do instead of playing on the computer.
> 3. Read the first page, drawing the student into the text so they will be keen to read the rest independently.
>
> **Shark for sale**
> 1. Ask the student to turn to p.31 in their Anthology.
> 2. Introduce them to the text 'Shark for sale'. Explain that this text is about buying something that turns out to be a bit different from the advertisement.
> 3. Read the advert on the first page, drawing the student into the text so they will be keen to read the rest independently.

Module 25

Jason's quest

Follow the timetable on p.55. Use pp.29–46 to teach the Speed Sounds lessons. The Module activities follow the same steps for every Module. These steps are outlined in the blueprint teaching notes (see pp.56–61). In addition to the blueprint teaching notes, some activities require Module-specific teaching notes, which are outlined below. Answers to some activities are also provided.

First Read

1. Story introduction:

> This text is based on a story from Greek mythology. The main character, Jason, longs to be the King of Greece. To prove he is worthy of this title, his father's brother, Pelias (*pel-y-us*) sends him on a mission. Jason must sail to the kingdom of Colchis (*col-kiss*) and bring back the Golden Fleece. The fleece is made from golden hair and is a sign of authority. The fleece is not only protected by a dragon, but Jason must fight off Harpies (birds with human faces), armies of soldiers, Sirens (female creatures that lure sailors to danger), and escape a whirlpool before he gets to the fleece. Is Jason brave enough to succeed? Will he and his trusted sailors, the Argonauts, achieve their task?

2. Introductory question: Have you ever had to carry out a difficult task you didn't think you could achieve? Did you succeed in the end?

3–6. Follow the remaining steps on p.58.

❓ Questions to Talk About

Note: This activity is only for small-group teaching.

Fastest Finger	What was Jason's quest? (Section 1)
Fastest Finger	Why was this going to be difficult? (Section 1)
Have a Think	Why was the king of the distant land weak and frail? (Section 2)
Read with Expression	How did the king of Colchis feel about the theft of the fleece? (*furious, outraged, aggressive*) Read aloud Sections 3 and 4, showing the king's feelings.
Fastest Finger	Who cast a spell to protect Jason and Medea? (Section 4 and 5)
Have a Think	Which episode in Jason's quest do you think sounds most exciting and why? (Sections 2 to 6)

Module 25

Spelling – Green Words

The completed grids should look like this:

	'best friends'	number of sounds		'best friends'	number of sounds
frail	ai	4	gloat	oa	4
roast	oa	4	sown	ow	3
approach	pp oa ch	5	sailed	ai	5
innocent	nn	7	gloated	oa	6
challenge	ch ll ge	6	speak	ea	4

root + ending	root	ending
protective	protect	ive
enlisted	enlist	ed

Hold a Sentence

When it was afloat, Jason loaded the boat and enlisted lots of sailors.

Proofread – spelling and punctuation

The correct text is: *The wicked king of that land groaned when he saw Jason and set him a test – to harness his fire-breathing bulls, and sow a field with dragons' teeth. He boasted that his test would be much too difficult.*

A Anthology – further reading

This Module links to the following texts on pp.35–43 of Anthology 5.

Left alone to die – The story of Alexander Selkirk

1. Ask the student to turn to p.35 in their Anthology.
2. Introduce them to the text 'Left alone to die – The story of Alexander Selkirk'. Ask them to talk about any stories they know about surviving on an uninhabited island (or people they have seen in reality TV shows or in films that have been left on an island).
3. Read the first page, drawing the student into the text so they will be keen to read the rest independently.

Extreme survival

1. Ask the student to turn to p.40 in their Anthology.
2. Introduce them to the text 'Extreme survival'. Explain that this text is a quiz to find out how well they would survive outdoors in the wild.
3. Read the first panel to the student. Ask them to predict how well they are likely to do in the quiz and explain why. Encourage them to complete the quiz independently.

Module 26

New boy

Follow the timetable on p.55. Use pp.29–46 to teach the Speed Sounds lessons. The Module activities follow the same steps for every Module. These steps are outlined in the blueprint teaching notes (see pp.56–61). In addition to the blueprint teaching notes, some activities require Module-specific teaching notes, which are outlined below. Answers to some activities are also provided.

First Read

1. Story introduction:

> Has anyone ever started your school halfway through the school year? Have you ever been the new boy or girl at school? Starting school after everyone else is very hard – most people have sorted their friendship groups and know their way around the school, which can make anyone new feel isolated and lost. This text is about 'new boy'. The boys in his class, Darren Hewitt and Stewart Sims, pick on him for being 'posh', and he doesn't have any friends to stick up for him. But an unfortunate football match changes everything.

2. Introductory question: What could you and your friends do to make a new boy or girl feel welcome?

3–6. Follow the remaining steps on p.58.

Questions to Talk About

Note: This activity is only for small-group teaching.

Have a Think	What did the new boy think about starting his new school? (*worried, nervous, embarrassed*) (Section 1)
Have a Think	What does Darren Hewitt think about the new boy? (*irritated, cross*)(Section 1)
Read with Expression	How did the new boy feel at first? (*lonely, unpopular, sad, isolated, scared, confused, hurt*) Read aloud the first part of Section 2, showing the new boy's feelings.
Read with Expression	How did Darren and his friends feel about the new boy after the lunch-time incident? (*unfriendly, they disliked him, felt mean towards him, despised him*) Read aloud the second part of Section 3, showing Darren's feelings.
Fastest Finger	How did the new boy's mum help Darren? (Sections 4 and 5)
Have a Think	Why does Darren say he will be the new boy now? (Section 5)

Spelling – Green Words

The completed grids should look like this:

	'best friends'	number of sounds		'best friends'	number of sounds
stew	ew	3	ambulance	ce	8
kn ew	kn ew	2	normal	or	5
ph ew	ph ew	3	hospital	none	8
snigg er	gg er	5	collect	ll	6

root + ending	root	ending
explained	explain	ed
wrecked	wreck	ed
blanked	blank	ed

Hold a Sentence

He pretended that he couldn't chew the stew so he spat it out.

Proofread – spelling and punctuation

The correct text is: *Dad could hear them too and he came down to the pond. "They sound like a right crew!" he said. I agreed with him. Anyhow, the grass was wet with dew and the boys were skidding. Darren Hewitt was running with the ball.*

A Anthology – further reading

This Module links to the following texts on pp.2–9 of Anthology 6.

Keep fit for footy

1. Ask the student to turn to p.2 in their Anthology.
2. Introduce them to the text 'Keep fit for footy'. Explain that it has tips about how not to get injured when doing sports.
3. Read the first page, drawing the student into the text so they will be keen to read the rest independently.

New school blues

1. Ask the student to turn to p.6 in their Anthology.
2. Introduce them to the text 'New school blues'. Explain that it is a short playscript, with different characters taking turns to speak. It is about a new boy being shown around a badly organised school. The main characters are the boy Andrew, his mother Mrs Gooch, and the headteacher Mr Booth.
3. Read the first page, drawing the student into the text so they will be keen to read the rest independently.

Module 27

Kevin the killer hamster

Follow the timetable on p.55. Use pp.29–46 to teach the Speed Sounds lessons. The Module activities follow the same steps for every Module. These steps are outlined in the blueprint teaching notes (see pp.56–61). In addition to the blueprint teaching notes, some activities require Module-specific teaching notes, which are outlined below. Answers to some activities are also provided.

First Read

1. Story introduction:

> The kids in Year 1 are allowed one pet to look after at school. They persuade their wonderful teacher, Miss Baker, to buy a hamster for the classroom. Miss Baker agrees and the class have a great new pet to play with. The kids call it Stan after their head teacher, who shares the same ginger whiskers! But when Stan starts to get fat, the kids wonder what's going on. Could it really be that Stan is just a good eater, or is there something else causing the hamster to swell?

2. Introductory question: If you could have any pet, what would it be? Why?

3–6. Follow the remaining steps on p.58.

? Questions to Talk About

Note: This activity is only for small-group teaching.

Fastest Finger	Why was the hamster called Stan? (Section 1)
Have a Think	What was the reason for Stan being so fat? (Section 2)
Read with Expression	How did Miss Baker feel about Kevin when he first escaped? (*alarmed, frightened, startled, scared, shocked*) Read Section 4 aloud, showing Miss Baker's feelings.
Have a Think	What did Kevin do with the lunch boxes? (Section 5)
Have a Think	Why do you think the dolls were glad when Kevin left the classroom? (Section 5)
Read with Expression	How do you think Miss Baker felt when she found Kevin in the arms of a policemen? (*relieved, glad, apologetic*) Read aloud Section 6, showing Miss Baker's feelings.

Spelling – Green Words

The completed grids should look like this:

	'best friends'	number of sounds		'best friends'	number of sounds
similar	ar	6	wire	ire	2
eager	ea er	3	actually	ll	7
target	ar	5	suppose	pp o-e	5
officer	ff er	5	gnash	gn sh	3
teacher	ea ch er	4	scratch	tch	5

root + ending	root	ending
suggested	suggest	ed
allowed	allow	ed

Hold a Sentence

Miss Baker chased him with her stapler, but he was much too fast for her.

Proofread – spelling and punctuation

The correct text is: *Miss Baker came rushing up, still clutching her stapler. "I'm sorry, officer," she said. "I know he looks a bit like a murderer, but he's quite sweet, really …" Well, she wasn't keen on Kevin, but she didn't want him to end up in the nick.*

> **A**
>
> ### Anthology – further reading
> This Module links to the following texts on pp.10–19 of Anthology 6.
>
> **The flight of Freddy Fish**
> 1. Ask the student to turn to p.10 in their Anthology.
> 2. Introduce them to the text 'The flight of Freddy Fish'. Explain that this is a comic strip story about a goldfish who plans to escape from his goldfish bowl.
> 3. Read the first page, drawing the student into the text so they will be keen to read the rest independently.
>
> **The dog ate my homework!**
> 1. Ask the student to turn to p.15 in their Anthology.
> 2. Introduce them to the text 'The dog ate my homework!'. Explain that this text is another comic strip story, this time about how a family cat leads a new puppy into trouble.
> 3. Read the first page, drawing the student into the text so they will be keen to read the wrest independently.

Module 28

Il Bello

Follow the timetable on p.55. Use pp.29–46 to teach the Speed Sounds lessons. The Module activities follow the same steps for every Module. These steps are outlined in the blueprint teaching notes (see pp.56–61). In addition to the blueprint teaching notes, some activities require Module-specific teaching notes, which are outlined below. Answers to some activities are also provided.

First Read

1. Story introduction:

> Have you ever been a spectator at a live sporting event? Have you or one of your relatives ever been involved in a live event? This text is about a sporting event in the city of Siena in Italy. The event is called the 'Palio' (*pal-ee-oh*). It is a very special horse race, where ten districts of Siena compete against each other to win the race. In the district of the Eagle, Bruno and his brother Lucca have been preparing for the Palio for months. Their Uncle Marco is the daredevil jockey riding *Il Bello* (*eel bello*), a handsome dapple-grey horse who has a good chance of winning. But is Il Bello victorious, or will a horse from another district beat him to the finish line?

2. Introductory question: If you could watch any live sporting event, which sport would you choose? Why?

3–6. Follow the remaining steps on p.58.

❓ Questions to Talk About

Note: This activity is only for small-group teaching.

Have a Think	What does Bruno think about as he strokes Il Bello? (Section 2)
Fastest Finger	How do the local people celebrate? (Section 4)
Fastest Finger	How did they change their buildings? (Section 5)
Have a Think	Why did Bruno think it would be difficult to describe the Palio? (Section 7)
Have a Think	Why were the riders described as courageous? (Section 7)
Read with Expression	What was the atmosphere like in the crowd? (*exciting, happy, noisy, thrilling, competitive*) Read aloud Section 9, conveying the feelings of the crowd.

Spelling – Green Words

The completed grids should look like this:

	'best friends'	number of sounds		'best friends'	number of sounds
ur ged	ur ge	3	miracle	le	6
struggling	gg ng	8	squ are	qu are	3
loyal	oy	4	relative	ve	7
decorative	or ve	8	massive	ss ve	5
triumphal	ph	8	village	ll a-e	5

root + ending	root	ending
families	family	es
quarelled	quarrel	ed

Hold a Sentence

The local people set up tables with candles in the middle and lots of food.

Proofread – spelling and punctuation

The correct text is: As he turned the bend, he crashed into several more horses and one of the jockeys was thrown into the crowd. Where was Uncle Marco? Bruno stood on tiptoe and scanned the runners with a frown.

Anthology – further reading

This Module links to the following texts on pp.20–27 of Anthology 6.

Life on a cattle ranch

1. Ask the student to turn to p.20 in their Anthology.
2. Introduce them to the text 'Life on a cattle ranch'. Explain that this text is about a modern day cowboy. Ask the student to talk about what they think a modern cowboy might do. (Clue: They live on cattle ranches!)
3. Read the first page, drawing the student into the text so they will be keen to read the rest independently.

Watch that turtle hurtle!

1. Ask the student to turn to p.24 in their Anthology.
2. Introduce them to the text 'Watch that turtle hurtle!'. Explain that this text is about different sorts of animal racing. Ask the student to talk about any races they can think of that involve animals.
3. Read the first two panels, drawing the student into the text so they will be keen to read the rest independently.

Module 29

A brilliant escape!

Follow the timetable on p.55. Use pp.29–46 to teach the Speed Sounds lessons. The Module activities follow the same steps for every Module. These steps are outlined in the blueprint teaching notes (see pp.56–61). In addition to the blueprint teaching notes, some activities require Module-specific teaching notes, which are outlined below. Answers to some activities are also provided.

First Read

1. Story introduction:

> This story recalls the real-life events that took place on the Siula Grande (*see-oo-la grand-a*) mountain in the Andes in 1985. The Andes are found in Peru in South America and make up the longest mountain range in the world. Only the most experienced and adventurous mountain climbers attempt to climb them. On this occasion, two British mountaineers, Simon Yates and Joe Simpson had successfully reached the summit of Siula Grande. It wasn't until they started to make their descent that the pair found their expedition hanging in the balance.

2. Introductory question: Have you and a friend ever been in trouble? How did you help each other out of the situation?

3–6. Follow the remaining steps on p.58.

Questions to Talk About

Note: This activity is only for small-group teaching.

Fastest Finger	What is the name of the mountain that Joe and Simon climbed? (Section 1)
Have a Think	Why was a broken leg like a death sentence on the mountain? (Section 2)
Fastest Finger	How far did Simon lower Joe, in stages? (Section 2)
Read with Expression	How do you think the two men felt once it got dark and things turned dangerous? Read Section 3 aloud, showing the fear and tension that the men must have felt.
Have a Think	Why did Simon cut the rope? (Section 4)
Read with Expression	What sort of man did Joe prove himself to be? (*tough, brave, strong, determined*) Read aloud Section 5, emphasising these qualities.
Have a Think	Would you have been angry with Simon for cutting the rope, if you had been on the end of it? (Section 7)
Fastest Finger	What is the name of the book that Joe wrote? (Section 9)

Spelling – Green Words

The completed grids should look like this:

	'best friends'	number of sounds		'best friends'	number of sounds
silent	none	6	treatment	ea	8
ledge	dge	3	descent	sc	6
experiences	ce	10	reluctance	ce	9
distance	ce	7	difference	ff er ce	7
weight	eigh	3	void	oi	3

root + ending	root	ending
assuming	assume	ing
achievement	achieve	ment
accidentally	accident	ly

Hold a Sentence

With their lives hanging in the balance, Simon reluctantly cut the rope.

Proofread – spelling and punctuation

The correct text is: *The descent to base camp was a distance of six miles. It took Joe four days, without any assistance. It was quite an achievement.*

A Anthology – further reading

This Module links to the following texts on pp.28–35 of Anthology 6.

Odd achievements

1. Ask the student to turn to p.28 in their Anthology.
2. Introduce them to the text 'Odd achievements'. Explain that achievements can be strange as well as impressive! Ask them what sort of odd achievements might be in the text.
3. Read the first two panels, drawing the student into the text so they will be keen to read the rest independently.

Emergency – the A and E department

1. Ask the student to turn to p.31 in their Anthology.
2. Introduce them to the text 'Emergency – the A and E department'. Explain that this text is a comical look at some characters who go to hospital with ridiculous problems. Ask the student if they can think of some silly reasons why someone might need a doctor.
3. Read the first two panels, drawing the student into the text so they will be keen to read the rest independently.

Module 30

Creature

Follow the timetable on p.55. Use pp.29–46 to teach the Speed Sounds lessons. The Module activities follow the same steps for every Module. These steps are outlined in the blueprint teaching notes (see pp.56–61). In addition to the blueprint teaching notes, some activities require Module-specific teaching notes, which are outlined below. Answers to some activities are also provided.

First Read

1. Story introduction:

> Have you ever heard of Frankenstein? Many people wrongly think that Frankenstein is a monster, but it is actually the name of the creature's creator, Dr Victor Frankenstein. The book *Frankenstein* was written by Mary Shelley in 1818. It follows the efforts of Dr Victor Frankenstein as he attempts to make a superior type of human being. He dedicates his life to the project and eventually finishes. However, Dr Frankenstein has not created the superior being he had hoped for. Instead, he is haunted by an unearthly, repulsive creature that fills him with horror – Frankenstein's monster!

2. Introductory question: Can you think of a great invention that helps you in everyday life? What does it do?

3–6. Follow the remaining steps on p.58.

❓ Questions to Talk About

Note: This activity is only for small-group teaching.

Fastest Finger	What did Victor hope his new creature would be like and in what way was he disappointed? (Sections 1 and 2)
Fastest Finger	What was the first evil deed the monster did and why? (Sections 3 and 4)
Have a Think	Why did Victor destroy the second creature? (Section 5)
Read with Expression	How did Victor feel when he heard Elizabeth's screams? (*aghast, horrified, full of dread and sorrow, determined on revenge*) Read aloud Sections 6 and 7, showing Victor's feelings.
Have a Think	How did the creature feel when he found Victor's dead body? (*remorse, guilt, sadness, despair*) (Section 7)

Module 30

Spelling – Green Words

The completed grids should look like this:

	'best friends'	number of sounds		'best friends'	number of sounds
revenge	ge	6	stitched	tch	6
savage	a-e	5	inventor	or	7
capture	ure	5	repulsive	ve	8
figure	ure	4	measure	ea ure	4
behaviour	our	7	ch ar ge	ch ar ge	3

root + ending	root	ending
injured	injure	ed
tortured	torture	ed
created	create	ed

Hold a Sentence

The idea filled me with horror but I had injured this creature.

Proofread – spelling and punctuation

The correct text is: *I went away to the mountains, to try to make a fresh start. But even there, my creature found me. The monster loomed out of the mist; his face a pale, sickly mask. He told me that yes, he had killed William – to punish me, his creator, for abandoning him.*

Anthology – further reading

This Module links to the following texts on pp.36–43 of Anthology 6.

Creature features!

1. Ask the student to turn to p.36 in their Anthology.
2. Introduce them to the text 'Creature features!'. Explain that this text is about how special effects are created in horror movies. Ask the student to talk about any scary movies they have seen (or movies that have a scary part in them).
3. Read the first two panels, drawing the student into the text so they will be keen to read the rest independently.

Monster

1. Ask the student to turn to p.41 in their Anthology.
2. Introduce them to the text 'Monster'. Explain that this is a poem written from the point of view of the monster that Dr Frankenstein created. Ask the student to talk about how the monster might feel about himself and his creator. Is it likely to be a happy/angry/excited/bleak/fun poem?
3. Read the first panel, drawing the student into the text so they will be keen to read the rest independently.

Module 31

Macbeth

Follow the timetable on p.55. Use pp.29–46 to teach the Speed Sounds lessons. The Module activities follow the same steps for every Module. These steps are outlined in the blueprint teaching notes (see pp.56–61). In addition to the blueprint teaching notes, some activities require Module-specific teaching notes, which are outlined below. Answers to some activities are also provided.

First Read

1. Story introduction:

> Macbeth is one of Shakespeare's most well-known plays. It is called a 'tragedy' play. A tragedy means that the story does not end well for some of the characters! This text is a summary of Shakespeare's famous tragedy. The play is about a Scottish Thane (a nobleman) called Macbeth. Macbeth and his wife, Lady Macbeth, will do *anything* to make him king. Soon, his jealousy and ambition lead him to commit the terrible act of murder. With the help of three hideous witches and their spells, one murder leads to another. Until one day, Lady Macbeth can't take it any more …

2. Introductory question: Can you think of another story where it doesn't end well for the main character?

3–6. Follow the remaining steps on p.58.

❓ Questions to Talk About

Note: This activity is only for small-group teaching.

Fastest Finger	Where did Macbeth and Banquo meet the witches? (Section 1)
Have a Think	What made Macbeth doubt the witches' prophecy about him becoming king? (Section 2)
Read with Expression	What was Lady Macbeth's reaction to her husband's fears after he killed King Duncan? (*reassuring, brisk, efficient, practical*) Read aloud the last two paragraphs of Section 2, showing her feelings and reaction.
Fastest Finger	Why did Malcolm flee to England? (Section 3)
Read with Expression	How does Macbeth feel when he sees Banquo's ghost? (*terrified, horrified, desperate, aggressive and vulnerable, confused*) Read aloud Section 4, showing Macbeth's feelings through the description.
Have a Think	Did Macbeth and Lady Macbeth enjoy their power and status? (Sections 5 and 6)

Spelling – Green Words

The completed grids should look like this:

	'best friends'	number of sounds		'best friends'	number of sounds
nervous	er ou	5	ridiculous	ou	9
vicious	ci ou	5	curious	ur ou	5
dangerous	er ou	7	obvious	ou	6
jealous	ea ou	5	ambitious	ti ou	7

root + ending	root	ending
dangerous	danger	ous
brutally	brutal	ly
suddenly	sudden	ly

Hold a Sentence

Lady Macbeth could not bring herself to commit the vicious murder.

Proofread – spelling and punctuation

The correct text is: *Tortured and haunted by their evil deeds, the Macbeths could not sleep or rest. They were suspicious of everyone and brutally killed their enemies.*

Anthology – further reading

This Module links to the following texts on pp.2–10 of Anthology 7.

Superstitions – sense or nonsense?

1. Ask the student to turn to p.2 in their Anthology.
2. Introduce them to the text 'Superstitions – sense or nonsense?'. Explain that this text is about superstitions and how some of them are very silly.
3. Read the first page, drawing the student into the text so they will be keen to read the rest independently.

A famous writer – Shakespeare

1. Ask the student to turn to p.6 in their Anthology.
2. Introduce them to the text 'A famous writer – Shakespeare'. Explain that some people think Shakespeare is the greatest writer who has ever lived. His plays are still read and performed all over the world today.
3. Read the first page, drawing the student into the text so they will be keen to read the rest independently.

Module 32

The invisible city

Follow the timetable on p.55. Use pp.29–46 to teach the Speed Sounds lessons. The Module activities follow the same steps for every Module. These steps are outlined in the blueprint teaching notes (see pp.56–61). In addition to the blueprint teaching notes, some activities require Module-specific teaching notes, which are outlined below. Answers to some activities are also provided.

First Read

1. Story introduction:

> This is an account of the eruption of Mount Vesuvius in Pompeii, Italy in AD79. When the volcano erupted, many thousands of people perished as Pompeii disappeared under the unstoppable lava. This text follows the story of a donkey and its owner, Paulus (*paw-lus*), who find themselves desperately trying to escape the doomed city.

2. Introductory question: What do you know about volcanoes?

3–6. Follow the remaining steps on p.58.

? Questions to Talk About

Note: This activity is only for small-group teaching.

Have a Think	Who is narrating (telling) the story? What relationship does Paulus have to the narrator? (Section 1)
Have a Think	What does the donkey think about the countryside he lives in? (Section 2)
Fastest Finger	What does he first notice that makes him feel uncomfortable? (Section 2)
Fastest Finger	What made him sure that something was definitely wrong? (Section 3)
Fastest Finger	Why did he lose control of the cart? (Section 4)
Read with Expression	How did the people and animals feel as the air grew dark and thicker? (*panicky, terrified, trapped, desperate*) Read aloud Sections 5 and 6, conveying the feelings of the people and animals.
Fastest Finger	Is this a true story? (Section 7)

Spelling – Green Words

The completed grids should look like this:

	'best friends'	number of sounds		'best friends'	number of sounds
responsible	le	10	predictable	le	10
edible	le	5	vegetables	le	9
capable	le	6	these	th e-e	3
uncomfortable	or le	11	graze	a-e	4

root + ending	root	ending
urging	urge	ing
probably	probable	ly
miserably	miserable	ly

Hold a Sentence

I trotted up the rough track with my cartload of wood, sniffing the crisp air around me.

Proofread – spelling and punctuation

The correct text is: *I thought things probably couldn't get worse, but they did. The air became so thick that it was almost unbearable, and it began to grow dark. Through the swirling, ashy clouds I could see the sea, heaving and thrashing uncontrollably.*

Anthology – further reading

This Module links to the following texts on pp.11–18 of Anthology 7.

A terrible day in Pompeii

1. Ask the student to turn to p.11 in their Anthology.
2. Introduce them to the text 'A terrible day in Pompeii'. Explain that this text is about the history of the Italian town Pompeii, which was buried when Vesuvius erupted, long ago. Ask the student to talk about what they think it must have been like to be living in Pompeii when Vesuvius erupted.
3. Read the first page, drawing the student into the text so they will be keen to read the rest independently.

Mission impossible!

1. Ask the student to turn to p.15 in their Anthology.
2. Introduce them to the text 'Mission impossible!'. Explain that this text is about a group of miners who became trapped underground. Ask the student to talk about the sort of problems the miners might have faced (lack of food, water, air, light, communication).
3. Read the first two panels on the first page, drawing the student into the text so they will be keen to read the rest independently.

Module 33

Penalty for piracy: Execution

Follow the timetable on p.55. Use pp.29–46 to teach the Speed Sounds lessons. The Module activities follow the same steps for every Module. These steps are outlined in the blueprint teaching notes (see pp.56–61). In addition to the blueprint teaching notes, some activities require Module-specific teaching notes, which are outlined below. Answers to some activities are also provided.

First Read

1. Story introduction:

> What do you know about pirates? Would you be surprised to know that not all pirates were men? This text is a short biography of two female pirates, Anne Bonny and Mary Read. Both women lived during the 17th Century and were extremely ambitious. They became fearsome and courageous pirates, but their adventures didn't last for long.

2. Introductory question: Do you know any other famous pirates (fictional or real)?

3–6. Follow the remaining steps on p.58.

Questions to Talk About

Note: This activity is only for small-group teaching.

Have a Think	Why were sailors scared of pirates? (Section 1)
Fastest Finger	Why did Anne's father disinherit her? What was Anne's revenge? (Section 2)
Have a Think	Why did Mary Read dress as a boy and then as a man? (Sections 4 and 5)
Fastest Finger	How did Anne and Mary meet? (Section 6)
Have a Think	What did Anne and Mary have in common? (Sections 6 and 7)
Fastest Finger	What did Calico Jack do when they were attacked? (Section 9)
Read with Expression	What sort of character was Anne? (*determined, aggressive, competitive, violent, fierce, physical, outspoken*) Read aloud Section 10, showing Anne's character in her words.

Module 33

Spelling – Green Words

The completed grids should look like this:

	'best friends'	number of sounds		'best friends'	number of sounds
determination	er ti	11	valuable	le	7
aggression	gg ssi	7	eighteenth	eigh ee th	5
preparation	ar ti	9	kn own	kn ow	3
dressed	ss	6	innocent	nn	7

root + ending	root	ending
traditionally	tradition	ally
co-operation	co-operate	tion
preparations	prepare	tion

Hold a Sentence

The government was determined to stamp out the pirates, who were stealing valuable cargoes.

Proofread – spelling and punctuation

The correct text is: *Mary married another soldier and they opened a tavern. Twenty years later, Mary's husband died and she made the decision to take a job as shipmate on a vessel bound for the West Indies.*

A | Anthology – further reading

This Module links to the following texts on pp.19–27 of Anthology 7.

Ballad of a pirate of distinction!

1. Ask the student to turn to p.19 in their Anthology.
2. Introduce them to the text 'Ballad of a pirate of distinction!'. Explain that this text is a ballad (poem) about a pirate called Whitebeard. Ask the student to talk about any pirates they know (e.g. Jack Sparrow, Long John Silver, Captain Hook, Blackbeard).
3. Read the first page, drawing the student into the text so they will be keen to read the rest independently.

Pirate application pack

1. Ask the student to turn to p.24 in their Anthology.
2. Introduce them to the text 'Pirate application pack'. Explain that this text gives information about applying for a job as a pirate. Ask them to talk about one good thing about being a pirate and one bad thing.
3. Read the first page, drawing the student into the text so they will be keen to read the rest independently.

Note that the final two texts in Anthology 7 are extended texts which the student will now have the reading stamina to read independently. The texts feature a range of characters from the *Fresh Start* Module and Anthology texts. Encourage the student to read them in their own time and as a celebration of how much they have developed as readers.

Timetable and Module activities for a small group

Timetable for a small group

If you are unable to teach one-to-one, you can teach students who have been assessed at the same level in a small group of up to four.

Follow the Speed Sounds lessons on pp.29–46, and the blueprint Module activities on the following pages, referring to pp.62–127 for Module-specific teaching notes, questions and answers.

Day 1	Day 2	Day 3	Day 4
Daily Speed Sounds lesson	Daily Speed Sounds lesson	Daily Speed Sounds lesson	Daily Speed Sounds lesson
Speed Sounds in Module	Partner Practice: Speed Words	Partner Practice: Speed Words	Spelling – Green Words
Module Green Word Cards	Red Word Cards	Second Read	Spelling – Red Rhythms
Partner Practice: Speed Sounds and Green Words	First Read	Questions to Talk About	Hold a Sentence
Red Word Cards	Read Aloud – Teacher	Questions to Read and Answer	Proofread
Partner Practice: Red Words			
Challenge Words			
Speeding up word reading (this is an extra activity if the students' word reading needs an extra boost)			

For homework activities and Anthologies, see p.61.

Module activities for a small group

Speed Sounds in Module

Turn to the Speed Sounds page in the Module (p.2). Some sounds are circled on the chart. These are Best Friends that need extra practice.

1. Explain to the students that all the sounds in a box are the same.
2. Using a Speed Sounds chart on the wall, point to and ask the students to read each circled sound in and out of order.
3. Include other sounds the students need to practise. Make it fun – get speedier as you point.

Module activities for a small group

▶ Module Green Word Cards

Turn to the Green Words in the Module (on p.3 in Modules 1 to 33). Gather the Module Green Word Cards for the text you are about to read.

Names and single-syllable words

For each word:

1. Ask the students to follow the routine: 'Best Friends, Sound Talk, read the word' (see p.134). Gradually, in later Modules, encourage them to read the word in their heads.
2. Say the word again, using pronunciation that gives meaning if possible. Ask the students to repeat.
3. Explain its meaning in the context of the story if it is an unfamiliar word.
4. Ask the students to read the word again.

Multi-syllabic words

The longer Green Words are divided into chunks (syllables) by a grey line.

For each word:

1. Hold the card up and cover everything but the first syllable. Ask the students to read the first syllable, then each part of the word. Only use the routine 'Best Friends, Sound Talk, read the word' if needed.
2. Show and say the whole word, tweaking the pronunciation if necessary, and using pronunciation that gives meaning, again where possible. Ask the students to repeat.
3. Explain the meaning in the context of the story if it is an unfamiliar word.
4. Ask the students to read the word again.

Root words and suffixes

For each word:

1. Cover the suffix. Ask the students to read the root word in Sound Talk.
2. Show the whole word with the suffix and ask the students to read it.
3. Say the whole word, tweaking the pronunciation if necessary, and using pronunciation that gives meaning, where possible. Ask the students to repeat.
4. Explain the meaning in the context of the story if it is an unfamiliar word.
5. Ask the students to read the word again.

▶ Partner Practice: Speed Sounds and Green Words

Partners have one Module between them. Ask them to turn to the Speed Sounds (on p.2 in Modules 1 to 33) and Green Words in the Module (on p.3 in Modules 1 to 33). They practise reading the Speed Sounds and Green Words. Ensure students point accurately underneath the sounds and words.

1. Partner 1 starts by teaching the Speed Sounds out of order using My turn Your turn (**MTYT**).
2. Partner 2 teaches the single-syllable Green Words out of order using **MTYT** and gives the meaning of each bold word.
3. Partner 1 repeats with the multi-syllabic words.
4. Partner 2 repeats with the root words and suffixes.

Module activities for a small group

▶ Red Word Cards

Turn to the Red Words in the Module (on p.3 in Modules 1 to 33). Collate the Red Word Cards listed and words from previous Modules that the students need to practise.

For each word:

1. Hold up the card, for example: 'said'.
2. Say the word and ask the students to repeat it.
3. Point to the card and say the sounds you can hear, *s-e-d* and then say *said*. Ask the students to repeat.
4. Point out the circled tricky letters 'ai'.
5. Ask the students to read the word again.

▶ Partner Practice: Red Words

Partners have one Module between them. Ask them to turn to the Red Words in the Module (on p.3 in Modules 1 to 33).

1. Partner 1 points to the words for their partner to read speedily.
2. Partners swap roles.
3. Repeat until students can read all the Red Words at speed.

▶ Challenge Words

Turn to the Challenge Words in the Module (on p.3 in Modules 1 to 33).

Explain to the students that the author needed to use a few extra words in the story with sounds that you have not taught them.

Write the Challenge Words on the board.

1. Use **MTYT** to read each word.
2. If they forget them while they read the story, you will tell them the word.

▶ Partner Practice: Speed Words

Partners have one Module between them. Ask them to turn to the Speed Words page in the Module (on p.9 or p.10 in Modules 1 to 33).

1. Partner 1 points to the words across the rows or down the columns, while Partner 2 reads them aloud. If a partner needs to Sound Talk a word, ask them to start the row or column again.
2. Swap roles.
3. Repeat until students can read all the Speed Words correctly without Sound Talk.

Module activities for a small group

▶ First Read

Partners have one Module between them.

1. Use the introduction in the Module-specific pages (pp.62–127) to introduce the text, without revealing the ending, to spark the students' interest.
2. Ask the students to discuss the introductory question on the Module-specific pages (see pp.62–127) with their partner. Then choose students to feed back their responses.
3. Ask Partner 1s to:
   - follow the words with their eyes while their partner reads the first section of the story
   - prompt their partner to Sound Talk any words they read incorrectly.
4. Swap roles on the next section. Continue to swap roles section by section.
5. Remind students who finish quickly to re-read the story. Swap who reads first.

Read Aloud – Teacher

1. Ask students to close their Modules.
2. Read the whole story to them, without asking for their help. Show your enjoyment.

▶ Second Read

Partners have one Module between them.

1. Partner 1 reads Section 1 of the story, then Partner 2 reads Section 2, and they continue to alternate until the end of the story. Students should not need to Sound Talk now, but should be reading with greater understanding and fluency.
2. The fastest readers can start the story again, with Partner 2 reading the first section.

▶ Questions to Talk About

Even though these are simple questions, below the students' comprehension level, they help the students notice what they've just read. You will find the questions on the Module-specific pages (pp.62–127).

1. Read out the questions. Do not ask the students to read the questions as many words are not decodable.
2. For each question, direct the students to the correct section to find the answer.
3. For Fastest Finger questions, ask students to find the answer in the text and point to it. For Have a Think and Read with Expression questions, ask them to discuss the questions with their partner.
4. Take feedback.

▶ Questions to Read and Answer

Turn to the Questions to Read and Answer page in the Module (on p.8 or p.9 in Modules 1 to 33).

1. Show partners how to take turns to read the questions and then, together, find and discuss the answers in the text.
2. Take feedback.

Module activities for a small group

▶ Spelling – Green Words

Turn to the Spelling page in the Module (on p.7 or p.8 in Modules 1 to 33).

1. Show how you complete a couple of words on the first grid. You could use the board to do this. Then then ask the students to complete. Support only if needed.
   - Column 1: Dot the single letters and underline Best Friends
   - Column 2: Write the Best Friends – if there are any
   - Column 3: Write the number of sounds
2. Show how you complete the second grid. Explain how to split the word into the root and suffix.
3. After completing the grids, ask students to check their answers with their partner.
4. Then go through the answers together as a group, ticking or correcting the Best Friends and the number of sounds.

The completed grids are provided in the Module-specific pages on pp.62–127.

▶ Spelling – Red Rhythms

Turn to the Spelling page in the Module (on p.7 or p.8 in Modules 1 to 33). Write each Red Word on the board to teach.

1. Ask the students to read the first word, for example: *said*.
2. Read the word in sounds: *s-e-d*.
3. Remind the students which sound the circled letter/s represents: 'ai' represents the sound *e*.
4. Point to each sound as you say the letter name/s in a rhythm (exaggerating the tricky letters and then practise saying the rhythm together).
5. Repeat with each Red Word.
6. Hide the words that are on the board.
7. Ask students to write each word in their exercise book one-by-one.
8. Show the words again, then ask them to tick/correct the spelling of each sound.

▶ Hold a Sentence

These sentences use words that the students have read. You will find the sentences in the Module-specific pages (pp.62–127).

1. Say the sentence and use **MTYT** to ask the students to repeat it until they can remember it.
2. Ask the students to write it in their Module (on p.7 or p.8 in Modules 1 to 33).
3. After students have written the sentence, write the sentence on the board.
4. Ask the students to tick/correct each word and correct any punctuation.

Module activities for a small group

▶ Proofread

Turn to the Proofread – spelling and punctuation page in the Module (on p.8 in Modules 1 to 33).

1. Ask the students to follow as you read the sentences aloud.
2. Ask them to proofread and correct the sentences.
3. Ask students to discuss the corrections with their partner.
4. Ask the students to tell you the spelling errors, then tick/correct their work.
5. Re-read the sentences, exaggerating the sentence breaks and the effect of punctuation. Ask the students where they have placed the missing punctuation and then ask them to tick/correct their work.

▶ Speeding up word reading

Once the students can read a word in Sound Talk, we then need to encourage them to read the word in their heads. These steps help students who are reluctant to let go of vocal Sound Talk.

Read Speed Words

Write eight Speed Words from the Module onto cards.

1. Ask the students to read the words using 'Best Friends, Sound Talk, read the word'.
2. For longer multi-syllabic words, show how you work out the word by looking for Best Friends and identify familiar chunks, before you read the word.
3. Show the students how you read three words in your head, mouthing the sounds without speaking (maybe whispering to begin with).
4. Give the students all eight word cards to read (in mixed order). If they need more support, repeat step 2.
5. Muddle the cards and ask the students to re-read the words in their head, building speed each time.

Increase the speed

1. Show the students how to read three of the words speedily.
2. Give all eight word cards to the students to read. Repeat until speedy.

Challenge time

Only do this if the students read the last set speedily.

Choose five new words from the Module.

1. Ask the students to read the words in their heads.
2. Ask the students to read the five words speedily. Repeat.
3. Muddle the cards with the first eight word cards. Hold the cards and ask the students to read the words speedily.

Glossary

Best Friends

Best Friends are a combination of two or three letters representing one sound, e.g. *ck, sh, ph, ay, igh, a-e*. Ensure students always say the sound and not the letter names, e.g. *sh* not *s* and *h*.

Best Friends, Sound Talk, read the word

When reading Green Words, students identify the Best Friends first, read the word in Sound Talk, then read the whole word, for example: *sh, sh-o-p, shop*.

Challenge Words

Challenge Words are low-frequency words that include a low-frequency grapheme or one that has not *yet* been taught.

Fastest Finger

Use during 'Questions to Talk About' in order to find a simple (recall) answer within the text.

Grapheme

The written version of a sound.

Green Words

Green Words are words with common graphemes. They are always taught by sound-blending.

Phonics Green Words are used on cards during the Speed Sounds lessons.

Module Green Words are printed on p.3 of the Modules (or on the same page as texts 1–11 and on the adjacent pages to texts 12–17 in the Introductory Module). Some of these also appear on cards with definitions relating to the context of the Module.

Speed Words are Green Words placed in a grid (on p.8 or p.9 of Modules 1 to 33) for students to practise reading the words at speed without sounding out each word (although if they stumble on the words, they *will* need to sound them out first).

Have a Think

Use during 'Questions to Talk About' to ask students to think more deeply about an answer, or provide an answer that requires inference.

My turn Your turn (MTYT) signal

This silent signal is used when you want the students to repeat something after you.

- My turn: gesture towards yourself with one or two hands.
- Your turn: gesture towards the students with one or two open palms.

Explain to the students that this signal is yours and not theirs.

Red Rhythms

Red Rhythms are used to spell Red Words (see explanation below). Use **MTYT** to spell out the word using letter names, and place emphasis on the letters making up the tricky grapheme, e.g. say *said*, then say the letter names in a rhythm, 's-ai-d', exaggerating the tricky part **ai**.

Red Words

Red Words ('tricky words') are common words with a low-frequency grapheme, e.g.

- *said*: the sound 'e' is written with the grapheme **ai**
- *son*: the sound 'u' is written with the grapheme **o**
- *your*: the sound 'or' is written with the grapheme **our**.

The complete list of Red Words with the 'tricky graphemes' circled is on p.138.

Sound Talk

Sound Talk is saying the individual sounds in the words. To help students to read, the teacher says the sounds and then students say the word. For example, the teacher says 'c-a-t', students say *cat*.

Think out loud (TOL)

'Thinking out loud' shows students the thinking necessary to work something out. They can 'see' what you think and how you work things out – as if you have a thought bubble coming out of your head.

Try not to make it look too easy. Hesitate, ask yourself questions and ponder as you formulate an answer.

Simple Speed Sounds chart

Consonant sounds – stretchy

f	l	m	n	r	s	v	z	sh	th	ng
										nk

Consonant sounds – bouncy

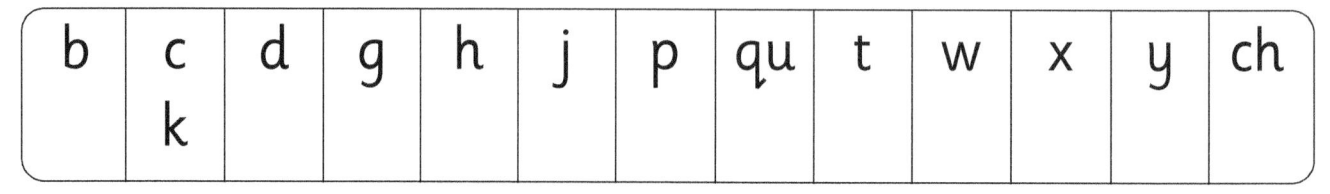

b	c k	d	g	h	j	p	qu	t	w	x	y	ch

Vowel sounds – bouncy

a	e	i	o	u

Vowel sounds – stretchy

ay	ee	igh	ow

Vowel sounds – stretchy

oo	oo	ar	or	air	ir	ou	oy

Complex Speed Sounds chart

Consonant sounds

f	l	m	n	r	s	v	z	sh	th	ng
ff	ll	mm	nn	rr	ss	ve	zz	ti		nk
ph	le	mb	kn	wr	se		s	ci		
			gn		c		se			
					ce					

b	c	d	g	h	j	p	qu	t	w	x	y	ch
bb	k	dd	gg		g	pp		tt	wh			tch
	ck		gu		ge							
	ch				dge							

Vowel sounds

a	e	i	o	u	ay	ee	igh	ow
	ea				a-e	e-e	i-e	o-e
					ai	y	ie	oa
					a	ea	i	o
						e	y	oe

oo	oo	ar	or	air	ir	ou	oy	ire	ear	ure
u-e			oor	are	ur	ow	oi			
ue			ore		er					
ew			aw							
			au							

Red Words

Red Words with circled graphemes

I th(e) y(ou) y(our) s(ai)d w(a)s
(are) o(f) w(a)nt wh(a)t th(ey) t(o)
d(o) d(oe)s (a)ll c(a)ll t(a)ll sm(a)ll
m(a)ny (a)ny (o)ne (a)ny(o)ne s(o)me c(o)me
w(a)tch wh(o) wh(ere) th(ere) h(ere) w(ere)
br(o)ther (o)ther m(o)ther f(a)ther l(o)ve ab(o)ve
tw(o) (o)nce b(uy) w(or)se w(a)lk t(a)lk
b(ough)t c(augh)t thr(ough) th(ough)t wh(o)le w(ear)
c(ou)ld w(ou)ld sh(ou)ld gr(ea)t
s(o)n w(a)ter b(a)ll
every(o)ne th(eir) p(eo)ple

N.B. The Introductory Module also contains the words 'my', 'me', 'no' and 'go' which are identified as Red Words in this Module. These become decodable later on in the programme so are not considered Red Words from Module 1 – instead they may appear in the Challenge Words list where the tricky sounds are still to be taught.

Summary of activity purposes

Activity title	Student's purpose
Reading activities	
Speed Sounds in Module	To practise reading the sounds in the text.
Module Green Word Cards	To practise reading the Module-specific Green Words and learn the meanings of new words.
Red Word Cards	To read the Red Words speedily.
Partner practice – Speed Sounds, Green Words and Red Words	To help our partners read the sounds, Green Words and Red Words.
First Read	To read every word in the text correctly.
Read Aloud – Teacher	To enjoy listening to the whole text.
Speed Words	To read the Green Words at speed.
Second Read	To read the text more speedily, without using Sound Talk.
Questions to Talk About	To find answers to questions in the text.
Questions to Read and Answer	To find answers to questions in the text and to write them down.
Anthology texts	To practise reading a variety of texts using the same Speed Sounds focused on in the Module.
Writing activities	
Spelling – Green Words	To practise spelling the new Green Words from the text.
Spelling – Red Rhythms	To practise spelling some of the Red Words from the text.
Hold a Sentence	To 'hold' a whole sentence in our heads before writing it down.
Proofread – spelling and punctuation	To correct spelling and punctuation errors.
Building vocabulary*	To explore an interesting word and to use it in our own sentence.
Grammar practice*	To focus on one aspect of grammar and use it in context.
Writing task*	To write a composition based on the text.

*Optional activities that can be completed at home.

Phonics practice activities for teachers

The six activities that follow will prepare you for teaching the programme. Work through them, preferably with a colleague so that you can help each other as you practise.

Terminology

In *Read Write Inc. Fresh Start*, the word 'sound' means 'the smallest unit of sound that we can hear or speak'. The word 'grapheme' indicates the written version of the sound.

    c-a-t = 3 sounds and 3 graphemes

  ch-a-t = 3 sounds and 3 graphemes

  l-igh-t = 3 sounds and 3 graphemes

c-r-a-sh = 4 sounds and 4 graphemes

s-t-r-ee-t = 5 sounds and 5 graphemes

'Green Words' are words made from the high-frequency graphemes shown on the relevant *Read Write Inc. Fresh Start* Speed Sounds poster. A grapheme can only be used to make up a Green Word when it has been taught from the poster.

'Red Words' are common words that contain low-frequency graphemes not included on the poster, e.g. 's**ai**d', 'w**a**nt', 'w**oul**d', 'b**all**', 'w**al**k'.

'Challenge Words' contain as yet untaught sounds that mean they are 'Red' until the grapheme has been taught – or they are less common words that contain low-frequency graphemes.

Sound Talk

Teachers need to know how to speak any single-syllabic word in pure sounds.

So: c-a-t = cat (say 'c' 'a' 't' not 'cuh' 'a' 'tuh')

Phonics practice activities for teachers

Activity 1: Learn to say the 44 sounds

Consonant sounds

Stretchy consonant sounds

Practise stretching each sound. (Avoid saying 'fuh', 'luh', 'muh', 'nuh', etc.)

ffff	llll	mmmm	nnnn	rrrr	ssss	vvvv	zzzz	ssshhh	ttthhh	nnng (thi**ng**)

Now say the shortest sound you can without an 'uh'!

f	l	m	n	r	s	v	z	sh	th	ng

Bouncy consonant sounds

Practise 'bouncing' each sound. (Avoid saying 'cuh', 'puh', 'tuh', 'chuh' etc.)

c-c-c-c k-k-k-k	h-h-h-h	p-p-p-p	t-t-t-t	ch-ch-ch-ch

Now say the shortest sound you can without an 'uh'!

c	h	p	t	ch

These are also 'bouncy' sounds, but it is harder not to say 'uh' – just do your best! Practise bouncing each sound.

b-b-b-b	d-d-d-d	g-g-g-g	j-j-j-j	w-w-w-w	y-y-y-y

Now say the shortest sound you can without an 'uh'!

b	d	g	j	w	y

Double consonant sounds

These sounds are actually two sounds made closely together, but they are counted as one.

x (c + s)	qu (c + w)	nk (ng + k)

(nk is paired with ng on the Speed Sounds poster)

Vowel sounds

The English language can be confusing, because there are only five vowel letters ('a', 'e', 'i', 'o', 'u') but twenty vowel sounds.

Practise saying each vowel sound in the accent used in your region.

a apple	e egg	i insect	o orange	u umbrella	ay day	ee see	igh high	ow blow

oo zoo	oo book	ar car	or for	air fair	ir girl	ou shout	oy boy	ire fire	ear hear	ure pure

Phonics practice activities for teachers

Activity 2: Learn to say words in Sound Talk

As a *Read Write Inc. Fresh Start* teacher, you will need to be able to say any single-syllable word in Sound Talk so that the students can learn to blend the sounds into a word.

The words in each of the rows below share a vowel sound, but may contain different vowel graphemes. Say the vowel sound first, and then say the word in Sound Talk. Touch a finger as you say each sound.

The number of sounds is printed after each word.

a	c-a-t 3	f-a-t 3	m-a-sh 3	s-p-l-a-sh 5
e	h-e-n 3	h-e-l-p 4	h-ea-d 3	b-r-ea-d 4
i	p-i-n 3	th-i-n 3	th-i-ng 3	th-i-nk 3
o	l-o-t 3	l-o-ng 3	l-o-s-t 4	p-o-n-d 4
u	h-u-t 3	j-u-m-p 4	c-r-u-s-t 5	j-u-s-t 4

ay	d-ay 2	m-a-k(e) 3	t-r-ai-n 4	
ee	g-r-ee-n 4	t-ea 2	h-e 2	k-ey 2
igh	n-igh-t 3	b-i-k(e) 3	t-ie 2	f-i-n-d 4
ow	s-n-ow 3	h-o-m(e) 3	g-oa-t 3	n-o 2
oo	z-oo 2	b-r-u-t(e) 4	b-l-ue 3	ch-ew 2
ar	sh-ar-k 3			
or	f-or 2	d-oor 2	s-n-ore 3	j-aw 2
air	s-t-air 3	c-are 2		
ir	g-ir-l 3	n-ur-se 3	h-er 2	
ou	ou-t 2	t-ow-n 3		
oi	b-oy 2	s-p-oi-l 4		
ire	f-ire 2			
ear	h-ear 2			
ure	p-ure 2			

More practice

d-ea-f 3,   ar-m 2,   l-e-g 3,   b-a-ck 3,   n-e-ck 3,   t-u-m 3,

sh-oe 2,   z-i-p 3,   v-e-s-t 4,   s-o-ck 3,   c-oa-t 3,   h-oo-d 3,

r-e-d 3,   b-l-ue 3,   b-l-ee-p 4,   b-l-a-ck 4,   p-ai-n-t 4,   p-e-n 3,   c-u-p 3,

r-u-n 3,   s-k-i-p 4,   p-u-m-p 4,   w-al-k 3,   th-i-nk 3,   s-m-i-l(e) 4,   s-i-t 3,

s-t-a-n-d 5,   l-u-n-ch 4,   s-ea 2,   b-r-ea-k 4,   h-o-m(e) 3,   ch-air 2,   l-igh-t 3,

w-a-ll 3,   t-oy 2,   b-oo-k 3,   b-a-g 3,   kn-i-f(e) 3,   f-or-k 3,

s-p-oo-n 4,   d-i-sh 3,   p-l-a-t(e) 4,   p-a-n 3,   b-r-ea-th 4,   j-a-m 3,

c-a-k(e) 3,   t-oa-s-t 4,   s-ou-p 3,   h-a-t 3,   ch-ee-se 3,   l-oo 2,   s-i-nk 3,

s-oa-p 3,   m-a-t 3,   t-a-p 3,   f-l-oor 3,   d-u-ck 3,   s-p-l-a-sh 5,

s-a-d 3,   c-r-o-ss 4,   g-o 2,   p-l-ea-se 4,   m-a-d 3,   g-l-a-d 4.

Phonics practice activities for teachers

Activity 3: Understand the Complex Speed Sounds poster

In each sound box on the poster there is one sound, but usually more than one grapheme.

Complete the charts below by adding the graphemes printed in bold in the following words. (The first two have been completed for you.)

Consonant sounds

photo be**ll** fu**nn**y stu**ff** pu**dd**le **wr**ap **kn**ow ho**rse** ca**rr**y cir**c**us pie**ce** bu**zz** **c**aution ho**bb**le s**t**i**ck** **ch**emist gi**gg**le bri**dge** bar**ge** **ge**ntle **wh**en li**tt**le gi**ve** ca**tch** deli**ci**ous to**pp**le

| f | l | m | n | r | s | v | z | sh | th | ng |
| ph | ll | | | | | | | | | nk |

| b | c | d | g | h | j | p | qu | t | w | x | y | ch |
| | k | | | | | | | | | | | |

Vowel sounds

m**y** t**ie** b**oa**t k**i**nd fl**ew** s**aw** d**oor** n**o** bl**ue** b**ur**n h**er** c**oi**n P**au**l sn**ore** br**own** m**a**ke b**i**ke h**o**me br**u**te happ**y** sh**e**

| a | e | i | o | u | ay | ee | igh | ow |
| | | | | | | | | |

| oo | oo | ar | or | air | ir | ou | oy | ire | ear | ure |
| | | | | | | | | | | |

Activity 4: Check what you have learnt about sounds and graphemes

- Look at the words below.
- Draw a dot under each one-letter grapheme.
- Draw a line under each two- or three-letter grapheme.
- Draw an arc to join each 'split grapheme' ('a-e', 'i-e', 'o-e', 'u-e').

For example: play shake

am and bad blot plan crib camp wind pond desk blend

grunt twist stiff press bluff thing spring drink splash

clutch slump stretch spray new boat tooth care stair

door make spark sprain brute bird spike law flight hair

need join out read furl bloke floor stone tie brown

bow joy fire hear pure

(See p.144 for the answers to this activity.)

Phonics practice activities for teachers

Activity 5: Read in syllables

- Read the words below in syllables. Say each syllable as it looks, not as it is pronounced, e.g.

    Mon|day choc|o|late pic|ture (as in pure).

Mon|day choc|o|late des|troy pic|ture pill|ow chil|dren
e|sti|mate sta|tion pa|tience temp|er|a|ture tol|er|ance

Activity 6: Count the graphemes in words with more than one syllable

- Look at the words below.
- Say each syllable as it looks, not as it is pronounced.
- Draw a dot under each one-letter grapheme.
- Draw a line under each two- or three-letter grapheme.
- Draw an arc to join each 'split grapheme'.

fo|llow con|cen|trate de|cide a|lone re|cog|nise bo|rrow
be|have a|mount croc|o|dile ex|tra|va|gant ac|cep|tance
dis|a|ppoint com|pare im|pa|tience dis|grace|ful be|cause
aw|ful de|li|cious ac|tion

(See below for the answers to this activity.)

Activity 4 answers:

am and bad blot plan crib camp wind pond desk blend
grunt twist stiff press bluff thing spring drink splash
clutch slump stretch spray new boat tooth care stair
door make spark sprain brute bird spike law flight hair
need join out read furl bloke floor stone tie brown
bow joy fire hear pure

Activity 6 answers:

fo|ll ow con|cen|trate de|cide a|lone re|cog|nise bo|rr ow
be|have a|mount croc|o|dile ex|tra|va|gant ac|cep|tance
dis|a|pp oint com|pare im|pa|tience dis|grace|ful be|cau se
aw|ful de|li|ci ous ac|tion